THE CRITICS DEBATE

General Editor Michael Scott

HAMLET

Michael Hattaway

MACMILLAN

For Sue, Ben, Rafe, and Max

© Michael Hattaway 1987

First published 1987

Published by
Higher and Further Education Division
MACMILLAN PUBLISHERS LTD
Houndmills, Basingstoke, Hampshire RG21 2XS
and London
Companies and representatives
throughout the world

Typeset by Wessex Typesetters
(Division of The Eastern Press Ltd)
Frome, Somerset

Printed in Hong Kong

British Library Cataloguing in Publication Data
Hattaway, Michael
Hamlet.—(The Critics debate)
1. Shakespeare, William. Hamlet
I. Title   II. Series
822.3'3   PR2807
ISBN 0-333-38523-3
ISBN 0-333-38524-1 Pbk

Contents

Acknowledgements

The author and publishers wish to thank the following who have kindly given permission for the use of copyright material: Associated Book Publishers (UK) Ltd. for 'On Shakespeare's Play; Hamlet' by Bertolt Brecht from *Poems 1913–1956*, eds. J. Willett and R. Manheim, trans. J. Willett, Methuen London, 1976.

Every effort has been made to trace all the copyright holders but if any have been inadvertently overlooked the publishers will be pleased to make the necessary arrangement at the first opportunity.

General Editor's Preface

OVER THE last few years the practice of literary criticism has become hotly debated. Methods developed earlier in the century and before have been attacked, and the word 'crisis' has been drawn upon to describe the present condition of English Studies. That such a debate is taking place is a sign of the subject discipline's health. Some would hold that the situation necessitates a radical alternative approach which naturally implies a 'crisis situation'. Others would respond that to employ such terms is to precipitate or construct a false position. The debate continues but it is not the first. 'New Criticism' acquired its title because it attempted something fresh, calling into question certain practices of the past. Yet the practices it attacked were not entirely lost or negated by the new critics. One factor becomes clear: English Studies is a pluralistic discipline.

What are students coming to advanced work in English for the first time to make of all this debate and controversy? They are in danger of being overwhelmed by the cross-currents of critical approaches as they take up their study of literature. The purpose of this series is to help delineate various critical approaches to specific literary texts. Its authors are from a variety of critical schools and have approached their task in a flexible manner. Their aim is to help the reader come to terms with the variety of criticism and to introduce him or her to further reading on the subject and to a fuller evaluation of a particular text by illustrating the way it has been approached in a number of contexts. In the first part of the book a critical survey is given of some of the major ways the text has been appraised. This is done sometimes in a thematic manner, sometimes according to various 'schools' or 'approaches'. In the second part the authors provide their own appraisals of the text from their stated critical standpoint, allowing the reader the knowledge of their own particular approaches from which their views may in turn be evaluated. The series therein hopes to introduce and to elucidate criticism of authors and texts being studied and to encourage participation as the critics debate.

Michael Scott

Preface

THIS IS not only yet another book about *Hamlet* but another book about books about *Hamlet*. It has eminent predecessors, including A. J. A. Waldock's *Hamlet: A Study in Critical Method* (1931), Morris Weitz's *'Hamlet' and the Philosophy of Literary Criticism* (1965), and Derick Marsh's *Shakespeare's 'Hamlet'* (1970), and, as it will in its time be supplanted, the customary apology is perhaps unnecessary. Waldock's chapters are devoted to critics (often an advantage); my first four to 'approaches' – a symptom of the integration of theory into literary criticism that has occurred during the last couple of decades. About this I feel ambivalent: I have no doubt that a critic must be methodical in his approach and that readers of criticism must learn to be able to deduce methods and ideological assumptions from the critical texts they read, if their authors have not 'come clean'. But theory notoriously can lead to abstraction, and 'ideas', by imposing a pattern on our literary experience, fail to illuminate not only particular passages of our play but also critical texts. I would not, I think, care to raise some of the abstruse ideas I have found most fascinating while writing this book with a director or actor at the Dirty Duck in Stratford-upon-Avon after a performance of *Hamlet*. So too the brevity of this volume has, I fear, tempted me into brisk or reductive accounts of some great pieces of writing. There are dangers of concentrating only on the 'point of view of a critic', and I hope that this book will serve to stimulate rather than foreclose further reading. All the authors I deal with will repay more thorough investigation – so will *Hamlet*!

The format of the series, however, suits my temperament as a critic and convictions as a teacher: that critical insight is gained only through a *plurality* of methods. There is no one key to *Hamlet*. All we writers can do is ask questions that are as informed and unmystificatory as we can make them. Answers can be found only in the rehearsal room by actors and directors, and these will be answers that are true only for that time and for that place (cf. Wittgenstein, 1966, p. 33). As I argue early in my text, not only is there no key to *Hamlet*, but there is no authentic *Hamlet*.

I have not attempted to read more than what I have sensed to be the most illuminating and accessible of critical works: to read many more would have turned this writer mad. I have concentrated on recent works, but have developed my accounts of them out of descriptions of classic *Hamlet* criticism. As this volume cannot be a comprehensive survey, it has seemed legitimate (and necessary to the continuity of my argument) to incorporate parts of my own thinking (and experience of the play in the theatre) into the arguments of Part One.

Quotations from *Hamlet* are taken from the text edited by Philip Edwards for the New Cambridge Shakespeare (Cambridge, 1985). I have had frequent recourse to the voluminous notes provided by Harold Jenkins in his edition of the play for the New Arden Shakespeare (London, 1982). Quotations from other plays by Shakespeare are from the Riverside edition (Boston, Mass., 1974). The system of references used in this series serves both to identify quotations and to indicate further reading.

My debts are many: Judith Hattaway, Sandy Lyle, and Howard Mills read my manuscript and rescued me from crass errors and many infelicities. I am principally grateful to first-year students of English literature at the University of Sheffield, who endured in the lecture theatre early reports on my explorations. Their reactions, critical and, occasionally, laudative, have improved the book no end.

Part One
Survey

Historical and formal approaches

IN THIS SECTION we examine the kinds of critical insight various forms of historical knowledge might generate.

In a famous phrase the Victorian critic Matthew Arnold defined the function of literary criticism as enabling the reader 'to see the thing in itself as it really is' (1911, p. 1). For a generation or so this century, many writers about literature, the so-called 'new critics', taking their cue perhaps from Arnold's use of the present tense in that phrase, tended to operate as though their task was simply to examine what they, as informed but not necessarily historically minded moderns, found in a text. They would describe formal and structural patterns, imagery, myths, textual ambiguities, assuming that these transcended the material or cultural conditions that obtained when the work was produced (see Ruthven 1979, p. 154ff.). They were, in general, a-historical. (Recently extreme claims for the validity of this kind of method have been made. It has been argued that if a reader can produce a reading of a text that is coherent or self-consistent, that reading need not be invalidated by the submission of historical counter-information. Meaning, critics who espouse the position would argue, is generated not necessarily by the effort of the writer in his time but, on the contrary, by the work of the reader in his. (See Ruthven 1979, p. 157ff.)

In what follows, I want to examine the ways in which knowledge of certain processes and phenomena from the past might help us understand our text, ways in which historical study might complement the approach I have just outlined (cf. McGann 1985; Belsey 1985). By stressing the difference between the age of Shakespeare and our own we are in fact questioning certain common cultural assumptions: the 'timelessness of great works of art' and the universality of those feelings and emotions that constitute an 'unchanging human nature'. Criticism based on such assumptions tends to depoliticise the play: by questioning them we remind ourselves that societies are open to change and, as we shall see later, *Hamlet* is peculiarly concerned not only with changes that are imposed upon the hero's world but also with his awareness of whether he might in turn impose changes upon that world. (In this connection we shall have to examine later whether or not it is possible to separate our knowledge of Shakespeare and his age from our assumptions as moderns.)

Is a text a thing?

To go back to Arnold: it might be assumed that the approach I am sketching in on the critical map would have as its goal 'to see the thing in itself as it really *was*'. But having offered that tentative hypothesis we must retreat from it, perhaps with some embarrassment. This embarrassment stems from the word 'thing'. Because today we generally encounter literature in book form, and because books are self-evidently 'things', we often talk about novels and plays as though *they* were things. The common 'new critical' pronouncement that we should concentrate above all on 'words on the page' surreptitiously implies that *words* belong in the same category as *pages*, i.e. that of things. Alternatively, we are sometimes encouraged to talk of poems as 'artefacts' or 'products'. As it happens, Shakespeare's plays were experienced not as things but as performances, processes rather than products, 'works' rather than 'texts'; moreover, much poetry of the period was heard rather than read and much was sung. Indeed, the notion of a poem or a play as a 'thing' does not in fact accurately describe our experience of reading a poem, let alone of seeing a play, because, unlike our experience of seeing a vase (or even a painting) – which is obviously a thing – our taking in of a literary work is not instantaneous but consists of a practice or activity that takes a measure of time. (We shall also reflect later on how *thematic* accounts of plays are oblivious not only of their particularity but also of our experience of them through time.) Moreover, as we shall see, the notion of a play as a *thing* does not match what we know of the processes of composition, publication, and theatrical realisation of plays in our period. There is no such 'thing', we may conclude, as *Hamlet*.

Textual criticism

We turn now to the first of our historically informed critical activities or methods. This is what is known as *textual criticism*. Its name may seem similar to 'practical criticism', but the resemblance is misleading: textual criticism is the study of the nature and transmission of manuscripts and printed texts.

Three early texts of *Hamlet* are extant (Edwards 1985, p. 9ff.). There is no manuscript: all are in printed form. The first (Q1) was published as a quarto – a smallish book about half the size of A4 paper – and is dated 1603. A reader familiar with the texts of the play that are published today would find this version of the play very strange: it is much shorter than the other two texts, and the part played by Polonius is taken by a character named Corambis. Familiar parts of the play appear in what seem to be severely mangled forms. It used to be thought that this was a first draft. Now it is recognised as a so-called 'bad quarto' – that is, a text that derives not from any authorial manuscript or from a manuscript associated with Shakespeare's company playing at the Globe, but from a 'memorial reconstruction' of the play that was made for performance. The principal agent in the reconstruction of the text seems to have been the player who took the part of Marcellus (for his lines are the least cut and garbled). It is reasonable to suppose that this text derives from a version prepared for a *provincial tour*. Q1 tells us a few things about the play as it was rendered in certain early performances: the Ghost appeared in the closet scene *'in his night gowne'* (so whetting Hamlet's awareness of his parents' sexuality?), Ophelia appeared for her mad scene *'playing on a Lute, and her haire downe singing'*, and when Laertes leaps into his sister's grave Hamlet *'leapes in after Laertes'* (sigs G2r, G4r, I1r). These are picturesque details in a text that is, like all early editions of Renaissance plays, tantalisingly short of such things, and it is tempting to assume that they are authentic. But of course they may not have occurred in performances in London. Indeed, if we are tempted to accept them into modern texts or performances we immediately confront the ideological question of why critics and historians tend to 'privilege' first performances over revivals, claim that the former are more 'authentic', and why they concentrate on performances in the metropolis rather than in the provinces. (The fact that Elizabethan players frequently went out on tour reminds us that their companies constituted not only a popular theatre but a true national theatre.) Modern experience of Shakespearean revivals indicates that productions by small companies on improvised stages can have qualities that elude far more prestigious ventures.

The Second Quarto, of 1604 or 1605 (Q2), derives from the author's *foul papers* (a technical term for his manuscript). It is the longest of the texts. But it is by no means unproblematic. As we might expect from a text that derives not from a playhouse but from the author's 'study' (if indeed Shakespeare had one), the speech prefixes (indicators of who is speaking) are not consistent and must therefore be regularised by modern editors. Certain stage directions are missing: we do not know, for example, whether Shakespeare intended Ophelia to exit before 'To be or not to be' [III.i.56ff.] or whether he thought of her 'overhearing' the soliloquy. (In a recent Prospect production the director, Toby Robertson, had his Hamlet, Derek Jacobi, deliver the speech while clasping Ophelia's knees like a child seeking comfort from its mother.)

The last of the texts, the Folio of 1623 (F) – it derives from the large-format collection of Shakespeare's plays that was made after his death – seems to be derived (but not directly) from a text that was prepared for *performance*. It omits 222 lines from Q2 but adds five new passages totalling 83 lines. It cuts the long speeches that lead up to the appearance of the Ghost at I.i.126 and I.iv.38, omits 27 lines of Hamlet with his mother, and a lot of Osric. Most significant, perhaps, is that most of the Fortinbras scene [IV.iv] goes – the scene which contains the 'delay' soliloquy ('How all occasions do inform against me . . . ') that has seemed essential to so many romantic critics of the play. (The passage in i.iv has also been overused by critics interested predominantly in personality.) Perhaps this text gives us Shakespeare's considered version of the play – we know from modern experience that first productions or first performances may not produce the best versions of new plays. Q2 may have been printed to resurrect his company's reputation after Q1 had been launched into the world, but the performing version was jealously guarded – companies often protected their playtexts by refusing to publish them.

The instability of 'Hamlet'

The existence of these three different texts raises immediately the problem of authenticity. Many people would assume that the 'authentic' is the 'original' – we believe after all (or most of us do) that Shakespeare wrote the plays attributed to him and that he was associated with the production of his plays and performed some of the functions of a modern director – there being no one to fill that role in the theatre companies of the English Renaissance (Hattaway 1982, p. 52ff.). But which kind of text is 'more authentic': one that derives from the study, or one that was presumably the result of work done in preparing the play for performance under the author's supervision? Should the dramatic meaning be 'privileged' over the theatrical one or *vice versa*? Both texts record plans for performance that were 'intended' by their author, but at different times. Recently textual scholars have given up trying to penetrate behind these two texts to reconstitute one ideal, eclectic text, because they realise that instead of Q2 and F being both relatively corrupt they both are relatively reliable: that is, they are records of different states of existence of the play. Moreover, we have seen from our study of varying texts that a Renaissance performance was constituted not only by the author but by certain social and economic factors in the culture he inhabited (McGann 1983). We know too from our modern experience that directors do not just follow the words that they find in a playtext but prepare it for performance: they cut and amend to give their production a shape which may be dictated in part by the forms and pressures of their time. On their side critics and spectators too will each experience the performance slightly differently. (*Hamlet* is a very long play and no one can retrieve all the parts of a play from his memory in the way in which the word-processor on which I wrote this book can retrieve all of the words I feed into its memory.) We said earlier that there is no such *thing* as *Hamlet*: now we can see just how an authentic *Hamlet* is an unrealisable ideal. We can put this another way and say that there are *texts* of this play but no *text*, just as in folk music or jazz there are *tunes* but no *tune*. As there are several early versions, there can be no easy logical connection between the 'original' and the 'authentic'.

We must now think further about the theatrical dimensions of a play. Some may say that there is no need to proceed further in this direction: we have a long version that derives from Shakespeare's study and a shortened version that comes from the theatre. We can note the differences between the two and feel that we are in full possession of a play by reading the eclectic versions that many modern editors give us, or by inspecting an edition with Q2 on one side of the volume's opening and F on the other. But I would argue that this way of experiencing *Hamlet* is still less than complete. First, because Shakespeare wrote for the theatre – and the reader of a playtext must be practised enough to reconstruct for himself the theatrical instructions which are inscribed in the printed text and thereby create a lot of the information the author of a novel or even a poem is able to supply him with directly. Ubersfeld (1978, p. 21) calls these 'didascalies' (cf. Dessen, 1984, p. 53ff.). (Should Hamlet force the king to 'drink off [the] potion' [v.ii.304], or is this a figurative description of another stabbing? Should he point to his head – or to the audience in the theatre – when he refers to 'this distracted globe' [i.v.97]?) An ideal reader must be aware of patterns and problems of staging, able to work out how formal a scene is, which lines are directed to which characters, which characters may be, even though they are silent, performing actions that serve to *tell* the audience more about what they are being *shown*. (Such devices create an ironical perspective on the action.) With so many indeterminate factors, every reader, however experienced or historically informed, will construct a different version of the play.

In modern texts, moreover, these *telling* details often appear in printed stage directions: Renaissance plays, however, were published – or have survived – without the lengthy descriptive commentaries or stage directions we find in the 'naturalist' plays of Chekhov or Shaw. Details of Renaissance productions are lost and are completely irrecoverable. We must remember, therefore, that it is conceivable that an early production contained pieces of business or stage action that modified the audience's perception of the text. *Telling* techniques – these include, of course, the conscious adoption of particular tones of vocal delivery – can alter our perception of moments when the author seems to be unobtrusive, simply *showing* us the story or, in a soliloquy perhaps, the 'character'. For it is often proper or effective for the action, *pace* Hamlet, to be *un*suited to the word [cf. iii.ii.15] (Weimann 1985). Something done by a player might usefully contradict what is said, or bring it about that certain lines which critics have been tempted to take as authoritative or choric – Shakespeare's own opinion on the matter in hand – are delivered ironically. 'Action is eloquence' as Volumnia said [*Coriolanus*, iii.ii.76], or, in today's critical idiom, representation implies re-presentation. Scholars who work on these Renaissance texts are like archaeologists confronted with the foundations of a great building. The words may be there, but the notation of spectacle and gesture, the great fabric of the production, is missing.

Hamlet is particularly beset by large problems of this kind: should we see Claudius on the stage as Hamlet sees him – is the king a drunkard and a lecher as well as a murderer? Is the Ghost to be presented throughout in a mode that will enable him to be affectionate towards his son as the Russian director Meyerhold saw him in 1934 (1969, pp. 279–80), or is he to be a wholly awesome figure who 'possesses' Hamlet – Trevor Nunn made the figure of superhuman size in his Stratford production of 1970. How should Gertrude comport herself during the play's second scene? Does the king see the dumbshow (Jenkins 1982, long note on iii.ii.423), and how exactly does Claudius react to 'The Mousetrap': should he look as if he had been seized by an apoplectic fit, as happened in the Olivier film, or might he stalk out in cool disgust, indicating the tastelessness of Hamlet's insinuation that 'the murderer gets the love of Gonzago's wife' [III.ii.239], as happened in Peter Hall's Stratford production of 1965?

We do not know whether Polonius was intended to be another conventional character, a sage counsellor (with a slight tendency to garrulousness when nervous), or whether he was to be a mouther of courtly platitudes (Frye 1984, p. 39). We do not know how far the stage tradition goes back of Laertes straining at the leash to get away from a father who advises him to be true to his 'own self'. Were the lines – a contrary interpretation this – intended to be, for the bright young law students who had crossed the river to see the play, an invitation to set down the *sententiae* they contained in their 'tables'? Should we take our cue from modern social and cultural historians and be inclined to see Polonius as a tyrannical patriarch who stamps on his children's affections, a mirror for all fathers out of sympathy with the romantic notions of marriage endorsed by the drama of the time (Wrightson 1982, pp. 89–120)? It follows that, as these crucial details that Shakespeare might have explained to the original players are irretrievable, we cannot validate an interpretation of the play by an appeal to the original as the authentic. We realise that in the case of *Hamlet*, as of all Renaissance plays, not only is there no authentic *text*, but neither is there any way of rendering a 'true' *performance* of any one of the surviving texts.

We must now enter yet another caveat. The text of *Hamlet* not only lacks crucial details of staging but the plot itself is notoriously full of loose ends. There are certain matters of fact that cannot be recovered: Shakespeare simply did not make things clear. We can react to these lacunae in two ways: first as evidence that Shakespeare did not revise his work sufficiently and left us a flawed masterpiece; or we might argue that they make the text interestingly ambiguous, one that is open to a range of performance possibilities, an 'interrogative' text (Belsey 1980, p. 91ff.), the meaning of which must be constructed by its readers and directors.

It is worth listing some of the traditional 'problems' of *Hamlet* at this stage. Previous generations of critics reacted to them as problems that had to be solved: now most would claim that these are questions in the play which might be *explained* but not *solved* by historical information, and that any resolutions will rest as much upon critical interpretations as upon historical 'facts' – and are likely to be pluralistic.

First, Hamlet's madness. In the last resort we do not and cannot know whether Shakespeare *intended* Hamlet to be played as a man whose madness was pathological, or whether his 'antic disposition' was a description, offered to friends, of actions that the prince, as a sane man, knew they might construe as those of a madman. In other words we cannot know whether Shakespeare intended Hamlet's actions to be clinically verifiable as being largely involuntary – which is the assumption made by those critics who argue that in Hamlet Shakespeare was offering a portrait of a melancholic man such as those described by other writers of his day. (Not that melancholy was a straightforward affliction. As Frances Yates asks, 'Is [Hamlet's] melancholy the inspired melancholy, giving prophetic insight into an evil situation and telling him how to act rightly and prophetically in that sitaution? Or is it a symptom of weakness like the melancholy of witches, making him prone to diabolic possession and the deception of evil spirits?' – 1983, p. 153.) My second example of a '*Hamlet* problem' derives from memories of a brilliant piece of theatrical invention in Robertson's Prospect production. Then, from her song, Ophelia threw the lines 'Quoth she "Before you tumbled me, / You promised me to wed" ' [IV.v.62–3] to Gertrude, thereby causing the Queen extreme embarrassment. Had Gertrude been unfaithful to Hamlet's father before the murder? Had she *thought* of being unfaithful? This is related to the question of whether or not she knew of the murder itself. Q1 adds to the closet scene the following for the Queen: 'But as I haue a soule, I sweare by heauen, / I neuer knew of this most horride murder' (sig. G2v). Did Shakespeare agree to this piece of explanation after players had perhaps pointed out a gap in the audience's understanding of the play's plot?

To these questions as to many others (these include the problem of whether or not Ophelia committed suicide, whether Osric was involved in a plot against Hamlet; whether Rosencrantz and Guildenstern knew the contents of the letter they carried to England; which was the speech that Hamlet wanted inserted in 'The Murder of Gonzago'; and even the age and presumed maturity of the hero – is he thirty, as the Gravedigger implies, or a much younger man?) there can be no answer.

Historical criticism, ideology and evaluation

If we cannot distinguish the true it may well follow that we are unable to pontificate about the good (Weitz 1965, p. 37). Until recently *Hamlet* was the most acclaimed of Shakespeare's plays. There are more references to it than to any other play in the years after its first performances and it was the play that obsessed, as we shall see, the romantic and post-romantic generations (Ingelby 1932, II, 540; Scofield 1980). Recently it has been displaced by *King Lear*. Its popularity would suggest that for a long time a high value has been put on the play. But this century there have been two famous dissenting voices: T. S. Eliot and D. H. Lawrence. Both rest their evaluations of the play on historical assumptions that may, however, derive from ideological positions.

Eliot concluded his important and provocative essay by branding the play 'an artistic failure' (1951, p. 143). He had made two assumptions, one (historical) that the *Hamlet* we now know is the reworking of an old play, and the second (critical) that the 'essential emotion of the play is the feeling of a son towards a guilty mother'. (It is impossible to separate off the purely historical from the critical or moral – although I shall deal with moral readings under 'Philosophical approaches'.) Eliot deduced this second contention from an observation that 'Hamlet is dominated by an emotion which is inexpressible because it is in *excess* of the facts as they appear'. It was impossible for Shakespeare to graft these (inexpressible) emotions onto the old play. Now we know that the 'unexplained scenes – the Polonius–Laertes and the Polonius–Reynaldo scenes' are not, as Eliot (following J. M. Robertson) thought, reworkings of an earlier version of the play. Does this invalidate his interpretation?

We can question the second contention too. Why should an 'emotion' rather than, say, an ethical proposition be 'essential' to the play? If we take the 'To be or not to be' soliloquy [III.i.56ff.] as being (as it probably is) a meditation not only on suicide but on action, we might argue that Hamlet is dominated by an awareness of the contraditions of his position, that he is confronted by what the Renaissance termed a 'case of conscience' (Rose 1975; Frye 1984, p. 182ff.): he may be damned if he allows Claudius to remain on the throne and damned if he swoops to murder him. (If we accept this argument we may be inclined to think that the problem of Hamlet's delay – considered as a symptom of his melancholy (Bradley 1957, p. 101ff.) – evaporates: theatrical time is needed to present the 'thinking . . . precisely on th'event' [IV.iv.41], the intricacies of Hamlet's case (but see Knights 1979, p. 57ff.).)

Dover Wilson contested Eliot's position with another historical assertion. Not only, he argued, was Gertrude guilty, but an Elizabethan audience would have agreed with the charge of the Ghost that she was guilty of 'damnèd incest' [I.v.83] (Wilson 1951, p. 43; Frye 1984, p. 77ff.) – significantly, however, Polonius makes no mention of this. Indeed the Bible does contain injunctions against marriage with a deceased husband's brother (Leviticus 18:16) and Elizabethans would have remembered the curse of childlessness (cf. Leviticus 20:21) that seemed to have descended on Henry VIII after he had married Catherine of Aragon, widow of his brother, Prince Arthur. Moreover, Dover Wilson reinforces his historical argument with a *critical* assumption that is, as we shall see, debatable: 'Shakespeare asks every spectator, every reader, to *sympathize* with his hero. . . . This is in part the meaning of the drama' (1951, p. 44).

Lawrence wrote on *Hamlet* in the course of describing several plays he saw performed in Italian in Garda. His brilliant essay (from *Twilight in Italy*, 1916) is partly shaped by Lawrence's meditations on his dislike of the histrionic and on the trust he placed on instinct as well as on notions of conflict between the sexes. Enrico Persevalli, who played Hamlet, disappointed and exasperated Lawrence. He went on to reflect,

I had always felt an aversion from Hamlet: a creeping, unclean thing he seems, on the stage, whether he is Forbes Robertson or anyone else. His nasty poking and sniffing at his mother, his setting traps for the King, his conceited perversion with Ophelia make him always intolerable. The character is repulsive in its conception, based on self-dislike and a spirit of disintegration.

Lawrence goes on to support his critical observation with some reflections on the period in which the play was written:

Except in the 'great' speeches, and there Enrico was betrayed, Hamlet suffered the extremity of physical self-loathing, loathing of his own flesh. The play is the statement of the most significant position of the Renaissance. Hamlet is far more even than Orestes, his prototype, a mental creature, anti-physical, anti-sensual. The whole drama is the tragedy of the convulsed reaction of the mind from the flesh, of the spirit from the self, the reaction from the great aristocratic to the great democratic principle.

An ordinary instinctive man, in Hamlet's position, would either have set about murdering his uncle, by reflex action, or else would have gone right away.   (1960, pp. 75–6)

Both Eliot and Lawrence focus on one aspect of the play, Hamlet's relationship with his mother (cf. Scofield 1980, p. 73ff.). They have chosen to place in the foreground this private part of the play at the expense of its concern with public issues, its anatomising of the Danish court, and its confrontation with matters of tyrannicide. (To be fair to Lawrence – and his essay above all other accounts resists summary – he implies that Hamlet is debilitated by his self-absorption, and the essay does go on to compare the body politic of the English Renaissance with that of ancient Athens, but the last two sentences I have quoted contain a disconcerting retreat from a central theme of the play, that of justice, to an airing of class prejudice.) In doing this these writers have taken up a critical stance that rests upon an *ideological* position: an assumption that private and familiar concerns are more important than public and political ones. (Having made that thundering pronouncement, I should like to retreat a little and concede that *Hamlet* demonstrates the inability of man to live by cause or idea alone. Action must be validated by instinct as well as by thought; the questions the hero faces are no mere abstractions but problems to be lived through.)

Ideology may be defined as a system of assumptions, practices and values by which a person lives and acts, or as a system which serves to legitimate a social order. (Its use is often to project sectional or class interests as though they were universal ones – Dollimore 1984, pp. 1–28.) It may be implicit rather than explicit in behaviour or discourse. Recently we have become aware that one of the tasks facing a reader of critical as well as literary texts is to examine the ideological assumptions of their authors. These may be crystallised as the reader confronts what he takes to be the ideology of the writer whose works he is describing. Ernst Honigmann has lately adduced an intricate web of evidence that adds new historical support to the contention that Shakespeare, like Donne, may have been brought up as a Catholic (Honigmann 1985). A writer who lived by this persuasion may be assumed to have been highly critical of many aspects of the regimes under which he lived, and may even have considered himself free from allegiance to a monarchy which, after the English Reformation, remained under papal interdiction (Frye 1984, p. 53). If we accept Honigmann's evidence and argument, need it follow that we should be inclined to see Shakespeare as a critic rather than an upholder of monarchical authority?

Even if a modern writer chooses to ignore issues of this kind, what he writes is likely to be informed by his own attitudes towards, say, this same issue of authority. Critics have often been teachers, authorities themselves in their students' eyes: is it not likely that they will appropriate their critical subjects to endorse their own positions? For a couple of generations critics assumed that plays tended to be supportive of the 'order' that, it was argued, was the basis of 'the' Elizabethan world picture (Tillyard 1943). They took small cognisance of the increasing rifts between city and court, of the system of censorship that had been developed to control the 'abuses' of players and writers, and forgot that, although it is possible to read Renaissance dramatic *texts* as being supportive of order, the institution of the *theatre* was by no means considered the ally of authority (cf. Bristol 1985). We can adduce evidence such as the following, which comes from a play written in the same year as *Hamlet*, Ben Jonson's *Poetaster*. Here Lupus, who occupies a position rather like that of Polonius, is complaining about the way in which he and his fellows are presented in the theatres:

> Indeed . . . these players are an idle generation, and do much harm in a state, corrupt young gentry very much, I know it; I have not been a tribune thus long and observed nothing: besides, they will rob us, us, that are magistrates, of our respect, bring us upon their stages, and make us ridiculous to the plebeians; they will play you or me, the wisest men they can come by still, only to bring us in contempt with the vulgar and make us cheap.   [I]

Too many modern critics, in other words, have been inclined to forget that plays can be, as Brecht considered, 'a reflection on rather than a reflection of social reality' (quoted in Eagleton 1976, p. 65).

It may be worth noting here that the play of *Hamlet* is resolved by the coming to the throne of a military strongman whose name, Fortinbras, suggests his nature. He is virtually nominated by Hamlet [v.ii.334–5] – as Hamlet was nominated by Claudius as his successor [iii.ii.309–10] – whereas Claudius was, according to the custom in Denmark, elected: Dover Wilson points out that Q2's stage direction at the beginning of i.ii which describes the assembly of characters in that scene as a 'council' (and which he takes to be authorial), indicates that the business of the scene takes place immediately after the ratification of Claudius' position (1951, p. 28). Now, for some people it is better to have a strong man than a good man as king: Machiavelli had dared to pose the question and Shakespeare's plays *Henry VI* and *Richard II* analyse it. Accordingly certain critics have inspected Claudius' first speech [i.ii.1ff.] and found his political acumen, his actions as a peacemaker (based on the strategic deterrents Marcellus describes in i.i.71ff.) and, moreover, his seeming kindliness to Hamlet to their liking. Very different opinions can emerge over the *style* of the speech: Howard Jacobson (1978) points to the macabre image of 'an auspicious and a dropping eye' [i.ii.11] (which may point to wry self-deprecation on Claudius' part?) while L. C. Knights finds here only 'unctuous verse rhythms' (1979, p. 32). John Bayley calls it 'suave, pacific, effortlessly cordial and yet formidably fluent' (1981, p. 167). On a more general level Wilson Knight wrote in 1930, 'Except for the original murder of Hamlet's father, the *Hamlet* universe is one of healthy and robust life, good-nature, humour, romantic strength, and welfare: against this background is the figure of Hamlet pale with the consciousness

of death. He is the ambassador of death walking amid life'
(1960, p. 32). This is (and was meant to be) a fairly
extraordinary claim. We cannot tell whether Wilson Knight
was thinking mainly about I.ii, which could be played in this
way, or whether he was simply repelled by the number of
deaths caused by Hamlet directly or indirectly as he sought
to scour the court of what he took to be its unclean elements.
(If we accede to this thematic opposition we must remind
ourselves yet again that there is no way of telling whether or
not the court was presented in this way in Shakespeare's
time.)

Now it is also the case that Wilson Knight's critique of the
play, like so many others, is couched almost entirely in moral
terms: he is working in the Arnoldian tradition that proclaims
poetry to be a 'criticism of life' (1941, p. 4). At its most
reductive this approach can be like the kind of history
practised in *1066 and All That*: it concentrates on whether or
not Hamlet was a 'good thing'. I would want to argue that a
moral reading – any reading that focuses on the moral
qualities of the hero measured on an absolute scale without
considering his role in a particular society – can only be
an incomplete reading (Knights 1979, pp. 186–200):
Shakespeare, it seems to me, was more concerned with rights
and wrongs than with good and evil. (This is the position
Wilson Knight defined splendidly in a later essay, '*Hamlet
Reconsidered*' – 1960, p. 298ff.) We must, accordingly, relate
the morality of the play to its ethics and its politics. Many
readings in the English tradition tend to suppress the political
(which is not to say, as I argued above, that they are not
political themselves). For I would claim that the 'essential' –
to use Eliot's word – problem of the play is that of a man
(whose sense of self is out of joint) seeking justice in a state
where the crown and court, the fountainhead of justice, are
themselves polluted.

Some historical questions

How did contemporaries of Shakespeare perceive the play?
We can begin by reminding ourselves that, as word meanings
have changed over the centuries since the play was written,

one of the first tasks for a critic is to be aware of the meanings particular words would have had for the play's first spectators. In fact it is probably impossible for even the most scholarly of readers to rinse the mind of inappropriate modern meanings – *Hamlet*, like any other text from the past, is covered, like a statue, by a patina that has formed as it has been 'corroded' by cultural and semantic change (Miller 1986).

Lexigraphical notes are necessary, but instead of terming them, as Dr Johnson did, 'necessary evils' (1960, p. 67), we might term them necessary preliminaries to the task of a responsible critical reading. Notwithstanding this, whole interpretations of *Hamlet* have turned on the meanings of particular words. When the prince says, 'Thus conscience does make cowards of us all' [III.i.83], is 'conscience' here defined by one of its early meanings – which in this context would have to do with awareness of all the complexities of the case – or is this faculty in Hamlet defined by 'ordinary modern usage, the inner voice of moral judgement? (Jenkins 1982, note on III.i.83; Frye 1984, pp. 132ff. and 179ff.). According to the one reading of this word – which occurs more often in this play than in any other tragedy by Shakespeare – Hamlet is pragmatic; according to the other, he is morally deliberative. The first line of Hamlet's first soliloquy – 'O that this too too solid flesh would melt' [I.ii.129] – contains a notorious textual crux: Q1 and Q2 read 'sallied', F reads 'solid'. The latter reading could mean simply that Hamlet was fat, that he thought of his flesh as too substantial to disappear, or could have to do with the congealing of a melancholic humour (Jenkins 1982, p. 437). 'Sallied' may mean 'assailed', in which case Hamlet, rather petulantly, describes himself as being put upon; Dover Wilson's emendation 'sullied' suggests that Hamlet morosely sees himself as contaminated – by his mother's (incestuous?) actions, as a consequence of Adam's sin, or by the visitation of the ghost? Does 'ecstasy', as I argue in Part Two, have a technical meaning, or is it simply synonymous with 'madness' as Edwards and Jenkins gloss its use at II.i.100?

A second kind of historical inquiry has sought to find prototypes for characters in the play in historical personages. So Hamlet has been described as 'a really detailed reflection of the inner [Earl of] Essex' (Wilson 1952, p. 104) or, far more persuasively, seen as playing the role of King James himself, who had been called upon to revenge the murder of his father, Lord Henry Darnley, by the Earl of Bothwell, who married his widow (Queen Mary) and himself became king (Frye 1984, pp. 31ff., 102ff.). (In the case of *Hamlet* there is no evidence external to the play to support any conjecture of this kind.) The limitations on the conclusions we can draw from hypotheses of this kind are, moreover, obvious: we cannot discover how many among the early audiences would have had the knowledge to make the identification, and we have no knowledge of any details of theatrical production that might have made the identification explicit.

Inquiry of this kind is of course dependent on what scholars can teach us about theatrical conventions. We know that Elizabethan players wore costumes that they had bought from the servants of courtiers – the courtiers having passed them on as some sort of payment in kind (Hattaway 1982, p. 86ff.). The original Claudius, therefore, may well have worn robes that would have invited certain courtiers to connect him with one of their number. In turn this line of inquiry leads to an investigation of the composition of Shakespeare's audience. How sophisticated were they? Was Hamlet himself correct in branding the 'groundlings' 'capable of nothing but inexplicable dumb-shows and noise' [III.ii.9–10] or was he simply revealing his own social squeamishness? (In a culture with comparatively high levels of illiteracy, the theatre, which communicates aurally, may well have been a channel of ideas, authoritarian or subversive, to intelligent but unlettered members of the lower orders of society – Hattaway 1982, p. 44ff. It is the noble Polonius, after all, who is 'for a jig or a tale of bawdry' [II.ii.458].)

A third kind of historical investigation can be pursued by studying Shakespeare's use of *sources*. In the case of certain plays Shakespeare followed fairly closely a printed text that is still extant (*Romeo and Juliet* provides an example), and it is possible by close comparisons to make informed guesses as to his intentions. *Hamlet* presents more complicated problems. Its source is a Latin chronicle by Saxo Grammaticus that Shakespeare seems to have known through Belleforest's French version. This was in some way grafted upon an earlier Hamlet play, now lost and probably by Kyd, that was being performed as early as 1589 (Edwards 1985, p. 1ff.; Bullough 1973, vii, 3ff.). The general problem with critical accounts of a text that derive from a study of its sources is this: should we emphasise the traces the source or sources may have left and thereby carry into the play assumptions, say, about the expectations original audiences may have had with regard to the genre of the source? Or should we, on the other hand, stress the innovations made by an author? Moreover, it is all too easy to apply a label such as 'crude' to any source without taking proper account of the place it occupied in the culture of its time. A 'primitive folk-tale' (Murray 1914) might have been constructed into a parable that was explosive to certain of its hearers.

A central source problem in *Hamlet* concerns the role of the Ghost. There is no ghost in Shakespeare's non-dramatic sources: do we assume that Shakespeare simply adapted the prose narrative for the stage, in which case the Ghost is 'merely' a theatrical device, familiar to Renaissance audiences from classical drama, for the rendering of inner experience, or do we take this innovation as central, a possible malign force, a spirit of evil whose nature infects that of the hero?

This question, to which we must return in another context, leads us to our fourth category of historical problems, that of the relationship between the content of the play and the 'ideas' of its time. *Hamlet* is much concerned, as we have seen, with the problem of revenge, and we must investigate this problem before we consider the nature of the Ghost, the dramatic instrument that impels the hero to avenge his murder. Revenge was a much-debated topic in the period (Frye 1984, p. 22ff.). The principal moral authority, the Bible, contains conflicting injunctions in different texts: the Mosaic laws of the Old Testament legitimise blood revenge for retribution, although they discourage vendettas. In the New Testament, we encounter a new gloss on the Old Testament text inscribed in Romans 12:19: 'Vengeance is mine, I will repay saith the Lord'. (The gloss to this chapter in the Geneva Bible urges a would-be revenger to convert rather than attack his adversary: 'For ether thou shalt wone him with thy benefit, or els his conscience shal bear him witnes y^t Gods burning wrath hangeth ouer him'.) St Paul goes on in the next chapter, 'Let every soul be subject unto the higher powers: for there is no power but of God: and the powers that be are ordained of God' (Romans 13:1). Now, if we interpret these texts as meaning that vengeance is the sole prerogative of God (and not as a promise that retribution is inevitable), then we have a maxim that is of great use to any prince plagued by feuds, duels, and political insurrections. He can deploy the biblical injunction as a means of social control, and declare any act of violence an act of rebellion against his authority. We find an example of this in 'The Homily against Disobedience and Willful Rebellion', one of the official sermons that was read regularly during the Tudor period in every church in the land. There rebels are identified with Satan, and it is argued that 'rebellion [is] worse than the worst government of the worst prince that hath been' (*Certain Sermons*, 1822, p. 511). The supposititious epitaph to the 'regicide' John Bradshaw (1602–59), 'Rebellion to tyrants is obedience to God' (cited in *The Oxford Book of Quotations*) offers a direct challenge to this sort of thing.

Certain (conservative?) critics of *Hamlet* have attempted to fix the meaning of the play by measuring the behaviour of the hero against homiletic maxims such as these which declare all revenge to be a sin, and have thereby concluded that audiences were not meant to approve of Hamlet and his actions (Prosser 1967). However, this kind of attempt to measure action against explicit moral and political codes is critically simplistic and historically reductive: sixteenth-century authors were sophisticating the problem so that a monarch's monopoly on justice was becoming – if not jeopardised – at least a matter for debate. In a celebrated record of Marlowe's table talk by Richard Baines we read, 'That all the apostles were fishermen and base fellowes neyther of wit nor worth, that Paull only had wit but he was a timerous fellow in bidding men to be subject to magistrates [rulers] against his Conscience' (Harleian MS 6848, fos 185–6). In more serious places distinctions were drawn between the revenge of public and private men and, if the object of the revenge was a prince, a distinction could be drawn between regicide and tyrannicide (Frye 1984, p. 30ff.). Instead, therefore, of just considering 'character', we must analyse situations.

Now, Hamlet's public status is ambivalent: although he is the heir-presumptive to the Danish throne, he is avenging a murder perpetrated upon his family. Moreover, Claudius appears to us as an efficient king, even if his confessional soliloquy makes us aware that he is far from being a good man – he cannot pray because he is not in a state to repent, being engaged in the planning of another murder (Frye 1984, p. 135ff.) – and all the evidence that would serve to brand him as a tyrant comes from the hero and the Ghost (if we agree that there is no indication in the text that Claudius ever definitively gives himself away). We must now re-examine the Ghost not only in the context of the play's sources but also in the context of Renaissance dramatic convention and pneumatology (the science of spirits).

Renaissance audiences would have recognised a ghost coming to encourage his revenger as a familiar dramatic and theatrical convention – we have only to think of the end of *Richard III*. In a commendatory verse to the collected works of Beaumont and Fletcher, Sir John Denham wrote in 1647 of the decline of drama after Fletcher:

> But now thy muse enragèd from her urn,
> Like ghosts of murdered bodies, doth return
> To accuse the murderers, to right the stage,
> And undeceive the long-abusèd age.

However, because Hamlet fears that the Ghost may be a demon in disguise, the matter has been seen as a theological problem which must be solved as a preliminary to determining the play's meaning. (For a robust attack on the 'ideas-of-the-time approach', see R. Levin 1979, pp. 153–6 and *passim*.) The text does at least confirm that the Ghost does not come from Hamlet's morbid fantasy – a notion that has been enacted in modern productions by portraying the Ghost merely as a disembodied voice, or by having Hamlet himself speak the lines in a different vocal register – because the Ghost is seen (but not heard) by Marcellus and Horatio. To his son he reveals that he had been 'confined to fast in fires, / Till the foul crimes done in my days of nature / Are burnt and purged away' [I.v.11–13], which accords with Catholic doctrine that ghosts were the souls of those trapped in purgatory (Thomas

1973, p. 701; Frye 1984, p. 19ff.). Reformed theologians denied the existence of Purgatory, and argued that apparitions could not be the spirits of the dead, which could go only to the undiscovered countries of heaven or hell. Ghosts that urged revenge were particularly suspect (Frye 1984, pp. 22–3). (The Counter-Reformation absorbed some of this teaching but argued that ghosts could be sent back to earth for special purposes – Thomas 1973, p. 703.) Accordingly, it has been argued, that to a reformed sensibility, the Ghost must have been a devil tempting the hero to an unholy course of action.

Hamlet himself is, of course, aware of the problem:

> The spirit that I have seen
> May be a devil – and the devil hath power
> T'assume a pleasing shape. Yea, and perhaps,
> Out of my weakness and my melancholy,
> As he is very potent with such spirits,
> Abuses me to damn me.
>
> [II.ii.551–6]

The play, however, offers no answer to the question of whether the Ghost is 'a spirit of health, or goblin damned' [I.iv.40]: Claudius' confessional soliloquy reveals that the Ghost spoke truth in that a crime of fratricide had occurred, but Horatio's final speech at least invites us to ponder whether the end of seeking justice justified means whereby deaths were 'put on by cunning and forced cause' [v.ii.362]. In the matter of the Ghost, we can certainly not, from the play alone, discover Shakespeare's doctrinal allegiance. (Perhaps Hamlet's demonising of the Ghost is another example of his prevarication: the Ghost may be, in other words, a psychological rather than a theological problem.)

What if there *were* some external evidence: say it could be proved without doubt that Shakespeare was a Catholic at the time he wrote *Hamlet*, or that he was familiar with an unequivocal statement about the origins of ghosts? Does it necessarily follow that in this matter Shakespeare should have followed the ideological teaching of any authority? Before we brand the Ghost as devil in disguise or instrument of the powers of justice, we must attend at least to the style of his speech – a topic much debated (Foakes 1973). If we were of the opinion that the majority of orthodox opinion favoured passive resistance over revenge, we might yet conclude that the majesty (at least at his first appearance) of this apparition spoke otherwise to contemporary audiences: art, after all, may as we have seen, not only reflect but challenge ideology.

Raymond Williams has written well about how in any one period there will be elements of dominant, residual, and emergent ideologies (1977, pp. 121–7), an observation that challenges and defeats the conventional view that there was one 'Elizabethan world picture' (Tillyard 1943). We might be able to be more certain about contemporary attitudes to its hero if it could be proved that *Hamlet* was written at the instigation of a particular court cabal, if we could relate the play not simply to 'ideas' but to ideas operating within particular institutions – but need Shakespeare have been loyal to this cabal? The play is designed in such a way that, although it opens onto some of the great questions of the age (James 1951), it aligns itself with none of the answers that were being offered, and certainly does not allow us to locate the author's view of these answers.

Formal approaches

There remains a final kind of historical study, that which compares the work with others that are similar in form. One line of criticism has related *Hamlet* to what is taken to be the 'purpose and method' of contemporary tragedy (Campbell 1930, p. 2ff.). This is taken to be the offering of examples to audiences of how to avoid becoming 'slaves of passion' and thus to avoid evil and misery. Such appropriation of tragedy by moral fable can only be exceedingly reductive. But *Hamlet*, we learn, belongs to a sub-genre: it bears obvious similarities to the so-called 'revenge tragedies' of the English Renaissance, plays such as Kyd's *The Spanish Tragedy* (1587?) and Tourneur's (?) *The Revenger's Tragedy* (1606). When we inspect the earlier of these plays, we discover a hero, Hieronimo, who is a sympathetic figure. Hieronimo seeks revenge for his son murdered by a political cabal from a court riven by corruption and intrigue and is driven to take justice into his own hands. Similarly Vindice, hero of the later play, seeks revenge by slaying the lascivious duke who had debauched and murdered his sister. According to a classic formalist critique, '*Hamlet* is in the tradition of revenge tragedy or heroic romance, a drama of intrigue, blood, and fate – a tradition derived from Seneca and sponsored in the Renaissance . . . in which the hero remains ideal (with no defect) throughout the play and attains his appointed revenge' (Stoll, cited in Weitz 1965, p. 48).

This kind of conclusion was rebutted by Eleanor Prosser (1967), who analysed all the revenge plays of the period and concluded that in the majority of them an Elizabethan audience would have been suspicious of a ghost and therefore unlikely to be sympathetic to the hero. Both cases depend on quantitative analysis of related plays; both fail logically because it is not necessarily the case that Shakespeare followed majority or dominant opinion (Powell 1980, pp. 42–3).

But we must go further and attend to details. In *The Revenger's Tragedy* Vindice calls for a sign from heaven:

> Is there no thunder left, or is't kept up
> In stock for heavier vengeance? There it goes!
> [*Thunder sounds.*]   [iv.ii.198–9]

At the climax of the play, in the masque of the revengers, the thunder sounds again:

> *The revengers dance; at the end, steal out their swords, and these four kill the four at the table in their chairs. It thunders.*   [following v.iii.41]

Now, there is no way of telling how we are to interpret this sound effect. Does it mean that Vindice is a scourge of God, fulfilling divine vengeance on the corrupt, or does it mean that God is showing his displeasure at a mortal who seeks to usurp his role as supreme judge? Is it a purely theatrical heightening of a play whose mode is that of pastiche? The sign is ambiguous. Likewise in *Hamlet* there is no sign, even though the hero, in a speech which creates an imagined antique (or antic?) and heroic role for himself, wishes that the thunder might speak for him as it spoke for Pyrrhus, his revenge hero from an earlier age:

But as we often see against some storm,
                . . . the dreadful thunder
Doth rend the region; so after Pyrrhus' pause,
A rousèd vengeance sets him new a-work,
And never did the Cyclops' hammers fall
On Mars's armour, forged for proof eterne,
With less remorse than Pyrrhus' bleeding sword
Now falls on Priam.
                                                    [ii.ii.441–50]

God remains hidden in the play, and Shakespeare seems to
be making it impossible for us to find in the play the kind of
moral certainty that Stoll derives from his construction of a
genre (Heinemann 1985, p. 219).

It follows that we cannot deduce a meaning for a work of
art from its form alone: we must consider all the particularities
of its content, its differences as much as its likenesses with
other similar works of its time. As Hegel asserted in *The
Philosophy of Fine Art* (1835) 'every definite content determines
a form suitable to it' (cited in Eagleton 1976, p. 21).

For reasons such as this I find myself out of sympathy with
interpretations of the play as myth or ritual (Fergusson 1953,
p. 109ff.). There are perhaps even more dangers in
'archetypal' criticism, which not only smooths over difference
but denies the work's historicity (Murray 1914). The 'very
age and body' of the play must be given its own 'form and
pressure'. As I shall argue in my own reading of the play, the
play's particular and unique structure – which offers us a trio
of avengers (Hamlet, Laertes, and Fortinbras, as well as
glimpses of a fourth, Pyrrhus) – invites each reader or
member of the audience to embark on a complex comparison
of the characters and roles of each. This work of comparison
will result *not* in a sense of 'pervasive unity, and an even
more profound resolution to the play' (Frye 1984, p. 5), but
in the awareness of discontinuity and discrepancy. The
common pursuit of meaning must be conducted, as in a
democracy, in a spirit of tolerance – and may very well not
lead to agreement.

Romantic and psychological approaches

Understanding this section depends upon grasping the distinction between 'romanticism', which is an ideology, and the period known as 'the romantic age'.

Ben Jonson, in conversation with William Drummond of Hawthornden, claimed that Shakespeare 'wanted art' (Donaldson 1985, p. 596); later the contention was to be erected into critical orthodoxy when Milton, in 'L'Allegro', contrasted Jonson's 'art' with Shakespeare's 'naturalness':

> Then to the well-trod stage anon,
> If Jonson's learnèd sock be on;
> Or sweetest Shakespeare, Fancy's child,
> Warble his native woodnotes wild.
>
> [ll. 131–4]

For many critics of the Restoration and eighteenth century, Shakespeare had lived in a rude, unrefined age. His rush-strewn stages were considered primitive compared with the new stages equipped for feats of spectacle (if not illusion), his language needed regularisation, the action of his plays violated unities and decorum, mingling kings and clowns, and his resolutions violated poetic justice, sacrificing 'virtue to convenience', as Dr Johnson wrote (1960, p. 33). His plays, as Garrick and his contemporaries thought, had to be adapted for performance (Davison 1983, p. 44ff.).

Romantic perspectives

The romantic critics, whose writings constitute a reaction to the positions I have just travestied in summary form, made three main contributions. The first was a new defence of the forms of Shakespeare's individual plays. Coleridge, thinking possibly of Voltaire's notorious disparagement of *Hamlet* as 'the fruit of the imagination of a drunken savage' (1749), sought to demonstrate that the judgement of Shakespeare was commensurate with his genius, that his plays did display art, and that they had a particular form of their own, an 'organic' form:

> The form is mechanic, when on any given material we impress a predetermined form, not necessarily arising out of the properties of the material. . . . The organic form, on the other hand, is innate; it shapes, as it develops itself from within, and the fulness of its development is one and the same with the perfection of its outward form.   (n.d., p. 46)

Secondly, and perhaps less happily for the course of Shakespeare criticism, this new way of defending the plays against neoclassical charges that they violated ideals of genre led to a new and idealistic conception of tragedy. The tragedies of Racine in France and post-Restoration tragedies in the English tradition – those, say, of Otway – had been concerned with matters of state, clashes between individuals and society: Romantic criticism tended to attend more to the spiritual agony and insight of the tragic hero. Tragedies became concerned with the transcendental, and the critics' search for meaning moved in the direction of a search for an ultimate order. Hegel wrote, 'From a purely external point of view, the death of Hamlet appears as an accident occasioned by his duel with Laertes, and the interchange of the daggers. But in the background of Hamlet's soul, death is already present from the first. The sandbank of finite condition will not content his spirit' (1975, p. 90). Coleridge noted that the Shakespearean drama grew out of the religious drama of the Middle Ages, and went on,

> If the tragedies of Sophocles are in the strict sense of the word tragedies, and the comedies of Aristophanes comedies, we must emancipate ourselves from a false association arising from misapplied names, and find a new word for the plays of Shakespeare. For they are, in the ancient sense, neither tragedies nor comedies, nor both in one, – but a different *genus*, diverse in kind, and not merely different in degree. They may be called romantic dramas, or dramatic romances . . . the romantic poetry – the Shakespearean drama – appealed to the imagination rather than to the senses, and to the reason as contemplating our inward nature, and the workings of the passions in their most retired recesses.   (n.d., p. 26)

This turning-away from institutions and history was not, of course, innovatory: Aristotle had argued that literature is more philosophic and general than history, and the eighteenth century, anxious to reinforce a hierarchy of genres, had made the leaden world of history inferior to the golden world of literature (Nuttall 1983, p. 66ff.). It was because he too was steeped in this tradition that Bradley, in what must be the most influential book on tragedy of our modern period, could write in 1904,

> Shakespeare's tragedies fall into two distinct groups, and these groups are separated by a considerable interval. He wrote tragedy – *pure* [emphasis added], like *Romeo and Juliet*; historical, like *Richard III*. . . . Then came a time . . . during which he composed the most mature and humorous of his English History plays (the plays with Falstaff in them). . . . But now, from about 1601 to about 1608, comes . . . Shakespeare's tragic period. (1957, pp. 61–2)

(Note the depoliticisation of the *Henry IV* plays by the concentration on the most 'rounded' and 'humorous' of their characters.) Recently *Hamlet* has been examined alongside such plays as *Measure for Measure* and *Troilus and Cressida*,[1] plays that the romantics consigned to the inferior category of 'problem plays' because they found in them evidence of sickness and decay in their characters. Since Ibsen and Shaw these plays have appeared in a new light: they are 'problematic' not because they refuse to adorn themselves in the familiar garbs of tragedy and comedy but because they address themselves to political and ethical problems and, what is more, resist 'closure', refuse to make their endings conclusions. (Certain modern productions have ended not with the hero dying sublimely, having transcended the political situation, but laughing ironically. This happened at Stratford in 1965 and in Robertson's Prospect production at the Old Vic in 1979.)

Thirdly (as is apparent from Bradley's defining parenthesis), romantic critics inclined above all to focus on the character – in its narrow sense of personality (contrast Brecht, cited in Dollimore and Sinfield 1985, p. 214) – of 'the tragic hero' (John Jones 1962, p. 12ff.: Lewis 1942, pp. 147–52). Hazlitt's great book was called *Characters of Shakespear's Plays* (1817), and the inclination soon set into a new orthodoxy: over a hundred years later, in 1930, the greatest Shakespearean

---

[1] E. M. W. Tillyard notes that he included *Hamlet* 'reluctantly' in his book *Shakespeare's Problem Plays* (1964, p. 1). Strangely, however, he addressses himself not to ethical problems but to those of religion and psychology. E. Schanzer's *The Problem Plays of Shakespeare* excludes *Hamlet* on the grounds that it 'lacks a central moral problem' (1965, p. 8).

director of his time, Harley Granville-Barker, was still writing, 'All great drama tends to concentrate upon character; and, even so, not upon picturing men as they show themselves to the world like figures on a stage – though that is how it must ostensibly show them – but on the hidden man' (1972, p. 7).

It is from this critical tradition that arises the – to my mind extremely reductive – habit of getting school children and, still, university students to focus almost exclusively on 'character': essays at this level are all too often merely a series of character sketches. This concentration on personality, the subject, is in fact an ideological assumption: it tends to rest on the myth of an unchanging 'human nature' (Belsey 1985, p. 2), defined in predominantly moral terms; neglects external realities and the ways in which individual consciousness or individuality may be a product of these realities; and thereby is oblivious to the possibility of political and social change. It ends by suppressing not only ethical awareness but even the possibility of studying the way an author makes words work, of learning about *characterisation*. Not surprisingly we find this conservative moralism inscribed in Dr Johnson's great 'Preface' when he was responding to Voltaire's charge that Shakespeare violated decency by making Claudius a drunkard:

> Shakespeare always makes nature predominate over accident; and, if he preserves the essential character, is not very careful of distinctions superinduced and adventitious. His story requires Romans or kings, but he thinks only on men. . . . He was inclined to show an usurper and a murderer not only odious but despicable; he therefore added drunkenness to his other qualities, knowing that kings love wine like other men, and that wine exerts its natural power upon kings.   (1960, p. 28)

(Johnson's approach can be defined against Marx's famous aphorism from the Preface to *A Contribution to the Critique of Political Economy*: 'It is not the consciousness of men that determines their being, but on the contrary their social being that determines their consciousness'.) Such an approach, as Johnson made explicit, ignores history. We might also contrast Brecht, who saw the play set between two ages, in a 'valuable fracture point' (Heinemann 1985, p. 207) between an archaic feudal world and the world of the Protestant

Reformation – Hamlet went to university in Wittenberg – where man had been taught to rely on reason and conscience:

> What a work this *Hamlet* is! The interest in it, lasting over centuries, probably arose from the fact that a new type, fully developed, stands out as totally estranged in a mediaeval environment that has remained almost entirely unmodified. The scream for revenge, ennobled by the Greek tragedians, then ruled out by Christianity, in the drama of *Hamlet* is still loud enough, reproduced with enough infectious power to make the new doubting, testing, planning appear estranging.
>
> (*Arbeitsjournal*, 25 Nov 1948, cited in Heinemann 1985, p. 217; Brecht's analysis of the final act of the play is to be found in Brecht 1964, pp. 201–2)

Looking at this another way, we might simply endorse the irony endorsed in a recent study by Jonathan Dollimore: 'Hamlet's brooding introspection does not achieve, but defeats, self-knowledge' (1984, p. 179).

Indeed, it is strange that so many critics have been obsessed with fixing Hamlet's character, getting it right, when, as we shall see in Part Two, the play is studded with references to contradictions within character, to the phenomenon of the divided, self-monitoring self. (Bradley does attend to the matter of the 'divided soul' but sees it as an essential condition of Shakespeare's heroes rather than as a response to particular circumstances – 1957, pp. 11–12.) It is for this reason that Hamlet may admire Lucianus, whose hands and thoughts are at one [III.ii.231], and perhaps why another riven soul, Claudius, finds much to admire in Lamort, a centaur figure exhibiting a perfect union of mind and body [IV.vii.84–7] (see Knight 1960, p. 319).

Character criticism

Let us now consider some more general limitations of 'character criticism'.

First, it tends to ignore role, the social being of individuals. 'The body is with the king, but the king is not with the body' [IV.ii.24]: in his antic riddle, addressed to Rosencrantz and Guildenstern, Hamlet is alluding to a contemporary theory of kingship that argued that the king was 'twin-born with

greatness' [*Henry V*, IV.i.234], possessed of a body natural
and a body politic metaphorically incarnate in the state
(Jerali Johnson 1967). As the fountainhead of power, the
king occupied a position of high visibility, high 'presence', as
he energised the nerves and sinews of the state. (The
metaphor emerges early in the play as Claudius describes his
relationship to Polonius by the analogy of the relationship of
head and heart, hand and mouth [I.ii.47–8]). He also,
according to another model of kingship, served as patriarch,
father to the kingdom. The crisis depicted in *Hamlet* derives
from the intersection and confusion of these two paradigms
of polity, 'public' and 'private', since, by challenging the
usurping father, Hamlet violates the mystical and 'divinely
hedged' [IV.v.124] body of the state (Barker 1984, p. 24ff.).
Accordingly the riddle sequence ends,

> HAMLET.   . . . The king is a thing –
> GUILDENSTERN.   A thing, my lord?
> HAMLET.   Of nothing.
>
> [IV.ii.25–7]

Putting this another way, we could say that Hamlet has a
specific task to do, and the execution of this task derives not
only from the hero's motives but from the consequences of
the actions of others. This makes it impossible to think of the
hero in simple moral terms: we must consider both his
situation and his experience. If Hamlet kills Claudius, in his
own eyes, perhaps, he restores justice, but this action of
revenge can equally be construed as murder (Belsey 1985,
pp. 112–16). By explaining Hamlet in terms of 'the heart of
his mystery' [see III.ii.331] alone, romantic critics explain
him away. 'Accounts of his unresolved Oedipus complex, his
paranoia – both clinical and vulgar – his melancholic nobility
of soul in a world made petty by politics have all served the
purposes of bourgeois criticism's self-recognition . . . have
. . . discovered . . . that alienated modern individual dejected
in the market-place of inauthentic values' (Barker 1984,
pp. 37–8).

Secondly, emphasis on character-as-personality tends to
elevate the 'individual' above the species, assume that
singularity or psychological complexity, especially if it is

accompanied by a high measure of self-consciousness, is of more interest than the typical – although Coleridge *is* good on the way that 'Shakespeare's characters are all *genera* intensely individualized' (Weitz 1965, p. 176). Hazlitt wrote,

> If *Lear* is distinguished by the greatest depth of passion, HAMLET is the most remarkable for the ingenuity, originality, and unstudied development of character. . . . The character of Hamlet stands quite by itself. It is not a character marked by strength of will or even of passion, but by refinement of thought and sentiment. Hamlet is as little of the hero as a man can well be. . . . The moral perfection of this character has been called in question, we think, by those who did not understand it. It is more interesting than according to rules; amiable, though not faultless. . . . His habitual principles of action are unhinged and out of joint with the time. His conduct to Ophelia is quite natural in his circumstances[!]. . . . Ophelia . . . is a character which nobody but Shakespear could have drawn in the way that he has done, and to the conception of which there is not even the smallest approach, except in some of the old romantic ballads. (1817)

Again Brecht's manifesto for his new kind of theatre may serve as a useful balance to this sort of thing:

> The new . . . theatre exposes any given type together with his way of behaving, so as to throw light on his social motivations. . . . Individuals remain individual, but become a social phenomenon. The individual's position in society loses its God-given character and becomes the centre of attention. (1977, p. 103)

Thirdly, too much of this kind of criticism ignores the material dimension of character we encounter in the theatre. Traditionally Hamlet serves 'purely as a character or role, never as an actor, always as the *product* of characterization, never as a process of bringing it out' (Weimann 1985, pp. 282–3). Yet even theatre directors, in their critical writings at least, can be victims of this myth of the ideal character. Harvey Granville-Barker wrote that a script is 'a score awaiting performance' (1972, p. 5). But the analogy is false: as we saw in the last section, we merely hear music whereas we hear and see drama. Musical notation can be very exact – not that it was in Shakespeare's time – but no one has yet provided an equally accurate notation for the performance of a play. Even crucial stage directions, as we have seen, are missing from Shakespearean texts. We go to

Hamlet several times in our lives, to see particular star performers, particular productions. We are likely to be pleased by the differences between these productions, whereas pleasing interpretation in music – with the exception of jazz, which is in revolt against the authority of the score – tends not to diverge from an 'ideal' or 'original' performance. So I would argue that a play is not merely realised in performance but transformed. We cannot really talk of Shakespeare's Hamlet; we can talk only of Gielgud's Hamlet, Burton's Hamlet (Davison 1983). We may be less willing to accede to the commonplace that the 'instinct of the actor is to identify himself with the character he plays' (Granville-Barker 1972, p. 25) if we agree that 'character' is not something fixed or stable. We might also be less happy about modern-dress productions of Shakespeare which are predicated on the principle of stable timeless characters unaffected by the material conditions of their age (Brecht 1964, p. 276; Heinemann 1985, p. 210ff.).

Fourthly, character-centred criticism tends to assume that 'character' is consistent throughout a play. This notion, of course, was critical orthodoxy among theorists seeking a simple didactic role for literature in the Renaissance and neoclassic period: the critic or historian should seek the 'inner causes' of actions which were in their turn attributable to one basic inclination or nature. Thomas Rymer went so far as to enunciate a 'rule' in 1678 that was to be taken up by Dryden and others. 'No simple alteration of mind ought to produce or hinder any action in a Tragedy' (cited in Dillon 1974). The German romantic Novalis wrote that 'character is destiny', and Coleridge noted that in Shakespeare 'interest in the plot is always . . . on account of the characters, not *vice versa* . . . the plot is a mere canvas and no more' (n.d., p. 54). Bradley's general position, which endorses this notion of determinate character, is stated in an argument of embarrassing circularity:

> The 'story' or 'action' of a Shakespearean tragedy does not consist, of course, solely of human actions or deeds; but the deeds are the predominant factor. And these deeds are, for the most part, actions in the full sense of the word; not things done ''tween asleep and wake', but acts or omissions thoroughly expressive of the doer, – characteristic deeds. The centre of the tragedy, therefore, may be said with equal truth

to lie in action issuing from character, or in character issuing from action. (1957, p. 7)

(To be fair to Bradley, in the case of *Hamlet* he does refine 'on the psychological analysis of his predecessors, attributing Hamlet's inactivity not to his native constitution but to an abnormal state of melancholy arising from shock' – Jenkins 1979, p. 22.) To the general argument, however, we might respond, 'Might not uncharacteristic action, what Horatio sums up as "unnatural acts" [v.ii.360] be more tragic? We have already seen how the play isolated the "divided self": may it not also deal with a "changing self"? Is Hamlet likely to be "himself" when his father has died and he is forced, probably for the first time, to consider the sexuality of his mother? Does he undergo a "sea-change" from melancholic to man of action after his fight with the pirates?' (Robertson economically hinted at this in his Prospect production by using emblematic properties: he had Hamlet carry about a mask he had picked up from the players until he departed for England, and then similarly take Yorick's skull from the graveyard through to the final dual sequence.) And we might point to two important speeches in the play that deal with fundamental change in men's natures. First, that of the Player King (Hamlet's inserted speech in 'The Mousetrap'?):

Purpose is but the slave to memory,
Of violent birth but poor validity,
Which now like fruit unripe sticks on the tree,
But fall unshaken when they mellow be.
Most necessary 'tis that we forget
To pay ourselves what to ourselves is debt.
What to ourselves in passion we propose,
The passion ending, doth the purpose lose.
The violence of either grief or joy
Their own enactures with themselves destroy.
Where joy most revels grief doth most lament;
Grief joys, joy grieves, on slender accident.
This world is not for aye, nor 'tis not strange
That even our loves should with our fortunes change,
For 'tis a question left us yet to prove,
Whether love lead fortune, or else fortune love.

[III.ii.169–84]

Secondly, that of Claudius where he talks of Laertes' love for his dead father (and also of his love for Gertrude – and even of Hamlet's love for Ophelia?):

> I know love is begun by time,
> And that I see, in passages of proof,
> Time qualifies the spark and fire of it.
> There lives within the very flame of love
> A kind of wick or snuff that will abate it . . . .
> [IV.vii.110–14]

These passages recall an essay, 'Of the Inconstancie of our Actions', by Montaigne, whose writings were certainly known to Shakespeare: 'We are all framed of flaps and patches and of so shapeless, and diverse a contexture, that every peece and every moment playeth his part. And there is as much difference found between us and our selves, as there is betweene our selves and other' (1910, II, 14). (Again we can compare Brecht: 'Even when a character behaves by contradictions that's only because nobody can be identically the same at two unidentical moments. . . . The continuity of the ego is a myth. A man is an atom that perpetually breaks up and forms anew. We have to show things as they are' – 1964, p. 15).

The fact that in both of the above speeches the character seems to be speaking 'for the play' as well as 'for himself' reminds us too that 'character' is not, in verse drama, given us by any kind of naturalistic representation (Weimann 1985, p. 282; Stewart 1949) or mimesis; that 'Hamlet' is a construct each of us, using intuition, imagination, and reason, makes from very diverse materials. As the Russian director Meyerhold wrote in 1915,

> May one not consider the tragedy of *Hamlet* as a play in which the tears are glimpsed through a series of traditional theatrical pranks? . . . In [this play] the elements of high drama and low comedy alternate not only in the play as a whole but within individual characters (particularly in the title role). In order to reveal this characteristic fully on the stage, we must construct the one kind of building where the actor will find it both easy and rewarding to *perform*. (1969, pp. 152–3)

The corollary of our awareness of inconsistency of character is that we shall be able to perceive how an audience watching a performance will not entertain a simple view of any one character but may swing between empathy and antipathy, identification and judgement. If we assume that the hero must be heroic or sympathetic, our 'identification' with him may lead us to view the whole action from a very restricted point of view. Bradley again: 'Both Brutus and Hamlet are highly intellectual by nature and reflective by habit. . . . Each, being also a "good" man, shows accordingly, when placed in critical circumstances, a sensitive and almost painful anxiety to do right' (1957, p. 63). Perhaps Bradley's inverted commas show some embarrassment at the consequences of his critical position: certainly his identification with Hamlet led him to trust the Ghost completely. A spectator who sees the play thus, from the point of view of a sympathetic hero, is forced to construct a villainous Claudius and Polonius.

Not only do critics in the romantic tradition look relentlessly for consistency, but they tend to explain character in terms of 'one-sided-ness, a predisposition in some particular direction. . . . In the circumstances where we see the hero placed, his tragic trait, which is also his greatness, is fatal to him. . . . [The] fatal imperfection or error . . . [in] Hamlet . . . is a painful consciousness that duty is being neglected' (Bradley 1957, pp. 13–15). The habit of reducing personality to formulae of this kind goes back to ancient times when it was held that personality or temperament could be explained in terms of the balance or imbalance, the 'complexion' [i.iv.27], of the four fluids or 'humours' – black and yellow bile, phlegm, and blood – which were to be found in the human body. The protagonists of French classical drama were created according to this recipe, and the notion of the 'ruling passion' was accorded much respect in the eighteenth century. Because Hamlet is obviously afflicted by grief and because he wears black, he has often (though the word 'melancholy' occurs only twice in the play) been described as a melancholic (Klibansky et al. 1964; Bradley 1957, p. 127ff.; Campbell 1930, p. 109ff. – on 'melancholy adust'), and his character 'explained' by reference to contemporary works such as Timothy Bright's A Treatise of Melancholy (1586), which was known to Shakespeare.

The sense that the 'one-sided character' provided an

adequate account of the hero was strengthened when a pseudo-Aristotelian theory of tragedy could be combined with Renaissance psychology. In a well known chapter of the *Poetics* (ch. xiii) Aristotle had described various kinds of plot, and concluded,

> The well constructed plot, must therefore, have a single issue. . . . The change of fortune must not be from bad to good but the other way round, from good to bad; and it must be caused, not by wickedness, but by some great error [*hamartia*] on the part of a man such as we have described, or of one better, not worse, than that.

The first thing to notice here is that there is no mention of a 'tragic hero' (John Jones 1962, p. 13ff.), and the second is that the word *hamartia*, which etymologically means missing the mark when shooting with a bow and arrow, designates an action: it does not designate an aspect of personality. However, by the time the Greek New Testament came to be written some 400 years after Aristotle's time, the word had changed its meaning and meant 'sin' (Wimsatt and Brooks 1957, p. 39). Thus, when Aristotle came to be translated in the Renaissance, the word tended to be applied to the nature of the 'tragic hero', and the familiar commonplace of the 'tragic flaw' – a notion much beloved of those schoolmasters who believe they are in continuous battle with the 'naturally wicious' – came into circulation. In turn this compound notion could be sophisticated by various psychologies: we can cite the best known (and reductively deployed) of these, Coleridge's character of Hamlet:

> Now one of Shakespeare's modes of creating characters is, to conceive any one intellectual or moral faculty in morbid excess, and then to place himself, Shakespeare, thus mutilated or diseased, under given circumstances. In Hamlet he seems to have wished to exemplify the moral necessity of a due balance between our attention to the objects of our senses, and our meditation on the workings of our minds, – an *equilibrium* between the real and the imaginary worlds. In Hamlet this balance is disturbed: his thoughts, and the images of his fancy, are far more vivid than his actual perceptions, and his very perceptions, instantly passing through the *medium* of his contemplations, acquire, as they pass, a form and a colour not naturally their own. Hence we see a great, an almost enormous, intellectual activity, and a proportionate aversion to real action, consequent upon it, with all its symptoms and accompanying qualities.   (n.d., pp. 136–7)

(For a useful account of how Coleridge's stress on the morbidity of Hamlet's personality has been neglected and how his various pronouncements on the play go far beyond mere 'character-criticism' see Ellis and Mills 1979.) I suppose that Olivier's sub-title for his film of the play, 'the tragedy of a man who could not make up his mind', is a reduction of this.

In our century Freud found in *Hamlet* symptoms of a morbid condition, a paradigm example of an Oedipus complex (1914; Ernest Jones 1949; Lidz 1975), a hero who was a hysteric, a man whose guilt over his repressed preoccupation with his mother's sexuality and passionate hatred of Claudius the father figure prevented him taking vengeance on his father's murderer. The notion was neatly inscribed in the 1980 Stratford production by John Barton. The stage was divided in two halves with costume skips and tailor's dummies upstage suggesting a rehearsal space. One of these dummies wore a suit of armour which resembled that worn by the Ghost. It was behind this rather than the customary arras that Polonius concealed himself in III.iv, so that, when Hamlet ran his rapier through it to kill the old man, he was also running through a figure of his father.

A modern Marxist critic, Arnold Kettle, however, offers clear reasons why he believes that this account does not take us to the centre of the play:

> the limitation of Freudian interpretations of the play is that, though they can throw light on the nature of Hamlet's experience and reactions – the effects on him of his father's murder (which he already half-suspects) and his mother's marriage – they tend to draw attention away from the real dramatic significance of that experience, that it makes him see the world differently in ways which have little to do with the experience itself. The personal crisis Hamlet has been through is the *occasion* of his new vision but does not explain it or help us to judge its ultimate validity. (1964, p. 150)

Now it might be objected that Hamlet himself offers us a model of the morbid or unbalanced tragic personality:

> So, oft it chances in particular men,
> That for some vicious mole of nature in them,
> As in their birth, wherein they are not guilty,
> Since nature cannot choose his origin,

> By their o'ergrowth of some complexion,
> Oft breaking down the pales and forts of reason,
> Or by some habit that too much o'erleavens
> The form of plausive manners – that these men,
> Carrying I say the stamp of one defect,
> Being nature's livery or fortune's star,
> His virtues else be they as pure as grace,
> As infinite as man may undergo,
> Shall in the general censure take corruption
> From that particular fault. The dram of eale
> Doth all the noble substance [often dout]
> To his own scandal.
> > [I.iv.23–38; 'dout' = put out, extinguish]

Although we may conjecture that Shakespeare jettisoned
these lines – they are omitted from the Folio text – critics
have made much of them (Campbell 1930, p. 22), and
Olivier extracted them to create an explanatory prologue to
his film. It is important to note here that Hamlet is talking
not about himself, the 'tragic hero', but about Claudius, and
that the speech is immediately followed by Hamlet's first
sight of the Ghost. The juxtaposition of speech and entrance
makes it tempting to read 'the dram of evil' (although the
phrase is a notorious textual crux) as a reference to the
Ghost, i.e. something external to the character.

Shakespeare does seem to have meditated upon the notion
of *hamartia*, to have considered whether the precipitating
action of a tragedy is an error or an action that is, in
Bradley's phrase, 'thoroughly expressive of the doer' (1957,
p. 7). The relevant passage comes near the end of *Coriolanus*,
where the hero's mortal enemy, Aufidius, is reflecting on the
nature and fortunes of his antagonist. (Coriolanus, a great
warrior, had incurred the wrath of a faction in Rome when
running for civic office and been expelled from his native
city):

> > First, he was
> A noble servant to them, but he could not
> Carry his honours even. Whether 'twas pride,
> Which out of daily fortune ever taints
> The happy man; whether defect of judgement,

To fail in the disposing of those chances
Which he was lord of; or whether nature,
Not to be other than one thing, not moving
From th'casque to th'cushion, but commanding peace
Even with the same austerity and garb
As he controlled the war; but one of these –
As he hath spices of them all, not all,
For I dare so far free him – made him feared,
So hated, and so banished: but he has a merit
To choke it in the utt'rance. So our virtues
Lie in th'interpretation of the time,
And power, unto itself most commendable,
Hath not a tomb so evident as a chair
T'extol what it hath done.
One fire drives out one fire; one nail, one nail;
Rights by rights falter, strengths by strengths do fail.

[IV.vii.35–55]

Aufidius' analysis is complex. First he offers a moral diagnosis (pride) of Coriolanus' character – but it is worth noting that this is seen as a disease (it 'taints' or infects), not as a birthmark (cf. Hamlet's 'mole of nature'). Then he offers the best translation of *hamartia* I know – 'To fail in the disposing of those chances / Which he was lord of'. Next he suggests that a man's nature might be defeated by a change in his external fortunes – but immediately refuses to be drawn into any moralistic conclusion since, he argues, each age will 'interpret' a man's strengths ('virtues') differently. The speech ends with a withdrawal from character altogether, and opens onto a Hegelian vision of tragedy as a collision of two self-validating ethical substances (Hegel 1975, pp. 46–51). The speech, therefore is sceptical of the possibility of finding any one model of personality as an explanation for tragic action.

I have quoted the speech at some length because it offers a coherent gloss on a semi-garbled explanation of his own conduct that Hamlet offers Laertes in some excitement just before their duel:

Was't Hamlet wronged Laertes? Never Hamlet.
If Hamlet from himself be tane away,
And when he's not himself does wrong Laertes,

> Then Hamlet does it not, Hamlet denies it.
> Who does it then? His madness. If't be so,
> Hamlet is of the faction that is wronged,
> His madness is poor Hamlet's enemy.
> Sir, in this audience,
> Let my disclaiming from a purposed evil
> Free me so far in your most generous thoughts,
> That I have shot my arrow o'er the house
> And hurt my brother.
>
>   [v.ii.205–16]

We are unlikely to accede to Hamlet's bad faith in claiming that it was his madness and not himself that killed his 'brother', but we may agree that a man taking arms against a sea of troubles as Hamlet had to do is unlikely to 'be himself'. We may even conclude that the figure, now familiar to us from our investigation of Aristotle, of the archer missing his mark with fatal results, helps us to understand this part of the play. We might also compare the archery imagery in the fourth ode of Sophocles' *Oedipus Rex*, and Montaigne's 'Of the Inconstancie of our Actions':

> No man makes any certaine designe of his life, and we deliberate of it but by parcels. A skilfull archer ought first to knowe the marke he aimeth at, and then apply his hand, his bow, his string, his arrow and his motion accordingly. Our counsels goe a stray, because they are not rightly addressed, and have no fixed end.   (1910, ii, 14)

(I am prepared to admit that my stress on the fragmentation or discontinuity of Hamlet's self is as 'ideological' [see above, pp. 20ff] as those critics with whom I find myself out of sympathy.)

This general approach tends to rest on the assumption that character is the sole cause, even the 'necessary and sufficient cause' of the tragic catastrophe. Now, plays are not like laboratory experiments: you cannot isolate a particular force and rerun the play to demonstrate that without that force the action would not have moved forward. Critics such as Bradley, who see the action as emanating from character are guilty of the logical fallacy of confusing explanations with descriptions (Weitz 1965, pp. 228–68). (Renaissance commentators would have been very unlikely to seek out one cause for the action; rather they would have thought in terms that derive from Aristotle's *Physics* and looked for four causes: final, efficient, formal and material – certain of which we should now term 'descriptions'. Thus, the final cause of Hamlet's death, the end for which he died, might be God's will inscribed in his 'special providence' [v.ii.192]; the efficient cause might be the duel that turns into a scuffle as the rapiers are exchanged; the formal cause the convention that in revenge plays the revenger himself is killed; and Hamlet's character is only one factor, 'the material cause'.)

Character-centred criticism is also likely to encourage its readers or spectators affected by it to think of the characters as real people. As romanticism evolved into realism in the nineteenth-century, a theatre for Shakespeare, creator of the greatest and most singular characters in Western literature, seemed to necessitate a building equipped to portray real places, a technological theatre that could create theatrical as well as dramatic illusion. (Coleridge at least recognised this distinction, noting that Shakespeare's own stages created illusion but not delusion – n.d., pp. 28–9.) However, the Renaissance playhouses that Shakespeare knew did not attempt theatrical illusion: there was no movable naturalistic 'scenery' and the players wore English costumes of the present, not foreign fancy dress of the past (Hattaway 1982, pp. 34ff., 86–8). There was no attempt to re-create 'Elsinore' on the stage – many names of the characters are, significantly, romanised rather than Danish. What was seen on the stage was never to be taken for reality: Elizabethan dramatists expected their audiences to be always conscious of the distinction between signifier and signified.

But let Dickens have the last word. In *Great Expectations*, Pip has been to see a performance of *Hamlet* that failed precisely because of its aspirations to theatrical realism:

> 'How did you like my reading of the character, gentlemen?' said Mr Waldengarver, almost, if not quite with patronage.
> Herbert said from behind (again poking me), 'massive and concrete'. So I said boldly, as if I had originated it, and must beg to insist upon it, 'massive and concrete'. (1965, p. 277)

Philosophical approaches

Romantic character criticism, as we have seen, tends to abstract character from the play. Let us attend once again to Coleridge, his comments on Hamlet's first soliloquy:

> O that this too too solid flesh would melt,
> Thaw and resolve itself into a dew. . . .
> [I.ii.129–30]

> This *taedium vitae* is a common oppression on minds cast in the Hamlet mould, and is caused by disproportionate mental exertion, which necessitates exhaustion of bodily feeling. Where there is a just coincidence of external and internal action, pleasure is always the result; but where the former is deficient, and the mind's appetency of the ideal is unchecked, realities will seem cold and unmoving. In such cases, passion combines itself with the indefinite alone.   (Coleridge n.d., p. 144)

Now Coleridge is perhaps making an acute psychological remark here and drawing attention to what, as we have seen, he considered to be a morbid element in Hamlet's personality. But many critics have, it seems to me, made the fallacious assumption that, because this morbid personality is seeking the indefinite, the play is in some way 'about' the indefinite. Or, often reductively, they have seen the play as explorative of themes, fairly abstract philosophical ideas – the interplay of truth and illusion, or the nature of a world or universal order. Donald A. Stauffer, for example, writes thus:

> This tragedy is impregnated with the intuitions of the bitter comedies that surround it – the death of something noble, the powerlessness of the good or the rational, the decay of that which was beautiful, the betrayal of trust, the savage insurgence of the base. Shakespeare had lost his belief in the building world of the English histories; the bright hope of the confident comedies had become clouded and overcast. Symbols for Shakespeare's brooding exist in Hamlet's situation: the majesty of the state murdered; the loyal, tender, loving queen debauched. The early positive ideas Shakespeare now consciously accepts as illusions – and on what is Hamlet's bitter cynicism based if not on his disillusioned idealism?   (1949, p. 125)

This passage is laced with illegitimate inferences about the state of Shakespeare's mind and his intentions, and assumes, wrongly I think, that a magniloquent abstraction is of more interest than description of a particular situation.

The perils of idealism

Now, I would argue that too much *Hamlet* criticism has been debilitated by thematic criticism of the sort inscribed in the above quotation, by its representative concentration on personal vision at the expense of objective thought, and by idealism. By that I mean the importation of ideas or ideologies (particularly notions of order) that are not direct products of the material bases and realities of the Renaissance and, more important, of the institutional structures created in the text. History – the ideas and institutions of a period – stands not just as 'background' in a text but is one determinant of its meaning.

Often, moreover, these ideas derive from notions of tragedy that themselves derive from structures of feeling that are remote from the experience some of us take from the play. As I argued in the last section, we must analyse the ideology, the ideas, values, feelings, by which we not only experience our society but also read the criticism of the texts that inhabit our culture. Tragedy is a form of narrative, and thereby a form of history. It is therefore an ideological assumption to call one form of tragedy 'pure' and another form, more evidently 'historical', 'impure' – or to argue that tragedy transcends history.

It happens that I myself am sceptical of any account of the play that shows the narrative being shaped, history being made, by a power or an 'order' that is not human. I believe that this text, like all the others in the canon, so aligns itself with this assertion that it makes sense to say that Shakespeare believed, with Machiavelli and Marx (1968, p. 96), that man makes his own history, although not necessarily in conditions of his own choosing. As Brecht wrote, all too many accounts of Shakespearean tragedy rest on the acceptance that what happens is fated, inevitable. This premise generates a particular kind of character, a passive and inevitably blinkered hero:

His character is built up by showing what happens to him. ... Lear reacts to the ingratitude of his daughters ... Hamlet to his father's demand to avenge him. ... The question is posed by 'fate', it only releases the trigger, it is not subject to human activity, it's an eternal question. ... The people act under compulsion, according to their 'character', their character is 'eternal', it has no causes that human beings can understand.   (Cited in Heinemann 1985, p. 213.)

Even if readers do not agree with this, they may concede, as I am about to attempt to demonstrate, that idealist approaches to tragic texts tend to be mystificatory.

We were concerned with some of the implications of Bradley's approach to the play in the last chapter. Bradley made no apology for mystification: 'Shakespeare was not attempting to justify the ways of God to men, or to show the universe as a Divine Comedy. He was writing tragedy, and tragedy would not be tragedy if it were not a painful mystery' (1957, p. 28; contrast Dollimore 1984, p. 53ff.). This frightening claim – compare Lawrence's remark that tragedy is a great kick at human misery – derives from the fact that Bradley was an arch-idealist. It is difficult to summarise his philosophy but it is something like this. (What follows is much indebted to René Wellek, 1975, pp. 85–103.)

Reality is one. All finite existence is 'a partial manifestation of the infinite'. 'Evil is the attempt at complete isolation of the part from the whole.' 'Spiritual forces struggle in the world: not abstract principles. These forces are embodied in men, often imperfect and even evil men who revolt against the order of the universe. But at the end, he believes, the moral order triumphs, harmony is reestablished.'

These ideas are obviously inscribed in the following key paragraph from *Shakespearean Tragedy*:

What, then, is this 'fate' which the impressions already considered lead us to describe as the ultimate power in the tragic world? It appears to be a mythological expression for the whole system of order, of which the individual characters form an inconsiderable and feeble part; which seems to determine, far more than they, their native dispositions and their circumstances, and, through these, their action; which is so vast and complex that they can scarcely at all understand it or control its workings; and which has a nature so definite and fixed that whatever changes take place in it produce other changes inevitably and without regard to men's desires and regrets. And whether this system or order is best called by the name of fate or no, it can hardly be denied that it does appear as the ultimate power in the tragic world, and that it has such characteristics as these. (1957, pp. 21–2)

Here fate becomes order, an extraordinary claim given the emphasis we have seen Bradley putting on mystery, and we can only deduce that this invasion of rational criticism by piety is due to ideology, an unstated and suprarational belief in Christian providence by Bradley himself. As Wellek explains,

> Tragedy is an image of this world drama and, Bradley argues, Shakespeare grasped this drama correctly, exemplified and reaffirmed it. Tragedy is [emphasis added] thus ultimately a *théodicée*, a defence of the world order. If, Bradley says expressly [in *Shakespearean Tragedy*], the world were 'the kingdom of evil, and therefore worthless', there would not be any tragedy, for nothing, neither suffering nor death, would matter greatly. Tragedy must be a collision of forces. The tragic hero is revolting against the order of the universe must perish but he must perish sublimely. 'We feel that this spirit, even in the error and defeat, rises by its greatness into ideal union with the power that overwhelms it' [*Oxford Lectures on Poetry*]. (1975, p. 87)

Bradley's argument is obviously circular – this spiritual conflict is an image of conflict in this world which is itself an image of the transcendent order – which leads to the extraordinary equation between 'order' and 'mystery' we have just analysed. (Bradley's view of the underlying thought of the play is in direct contrast to that of Rebecca West, who argues that *Hamlet* 'is as pessimistic as any great work of literature ever written' – 1958, pp. 17–32.)

This harmonic model of tragic resolution, moreover, does not fit most of the productions of *Hamlet* that I have seen. To take just two examples: the play ends not with union or what might be called 'harmonic integration', but with the coming to power of Fortinbras, a warrior king (Knight 1960, p. 324). In 1981, during the Solidarity period in Poland, Andrzej Wajda did a production that clad Fortinbras in the uniform of a Soviet Commissar – embarking on another raid on the Polish nation [see iv.iv.12ff.]. The production merely highlighted the discomfort that Hamlet himself has in the presence of this military adventurer. At the end of the play Fortinbras is to rule, OK? And does the soldier's music that he orders for the departure of Hamlet's body from the stage suit the prince's character?

Bradley's notion of tragedy derives from Hegel's paradigm of the synthesis after conflict of thesis and antithesis, rebelling hero and universal order. But why should the hero 'perish sublimely'? Our second example comes from 1965, when, at Stratford, Peter Hall's Hamlet (David Warner) died laughing, knowing only that the world in which order depends on the accidental switching of rapiers during a scuffle is as absurd as he thought it was when the play started.

Bradley's idealism distorts for me his whole reading of the play. He describes Hamlet's own idealism borne down by shock (1957, pp. 90ff.). What constitutes his idealism? Is he brave, honourable, driven by a high moral sense? Ophelia speaks glowingly of her prince, but then she would, wouldn't she? Bradley's Hegelianism allows him to assume that evil actions are the result of good intentions conflicting with an antithetical imperfect world; they will be synthesised into evil: 'man's thought, translated into act is transformed into the opposite of itself' (p. 20). He can write, therefore, that Hamlet, like Brutus, is a ' "good man" ' (p. 63) – perhaps the inverted commas betray some critical embarrassment. Hamlet's 'tragic error' is 'a painful consciousness that duty is being neglected' (p. 15) – but, as we have seen, Hamlet does not assume as Bradley does (p. 141) that his is the sacred duty of revenge, for, as he states, the Ghost may well be a goblin damned rather than a spirit of health [see I.iv.40].

Tragedies not 'tragedy'

The 'central feeling is the impression of waste' – this is one of Bradley's most celebrated descriptions of tragedy. Presumably most of us would accept that, but not perhaps the way he continues:

> With Shakespeare, at any rate, the pity and fear which are stirred by the tragic story seem to unite with, and even to merge in, a profound sense of sadness and mystery, which is due to this impression of waste. . . . We seem to have before us a type of the mystery of the whole world, the tragic fact which extends far beyond the limits of tragedy. (1957, p. 16)

We have already spoken of 'mystery'. Fear was one of the emotions Aristotle found in tragedy, appropriate in a culture that believed that its gods were all powerful but not necessarily moral, inappropriate to a play built upon Christian or humanist assumptions. As Auden remarked, Greek tragedy is the tragedy of necessity, Christian tragedy the tragedy of possibility (cited in Wimsatt and Brooks 1957, p. 55). A good production, moreover, might arouse not a sense of mystery but a sense of understanding – at least of the particular course through the text that the director had followed. This invocation of a mystical subject leads, it seems to me, all too often to mystificatory criticism. Critics feel, perhaps, that because they are in the presence of a 'high' genre – tragedy had been privileged over other forms of writing in neoclassical hierarchies (Sidney 1973, pp. 103, 117) – their prose should climb towards abstraction. (We might also label this retreat towards idealism as an example of *trahison des clercs* who retreat from analysis and action to the ivory tower of contemplation.) Here is another example:

> Shakespeare was in touch with something more than his age, and if we are ... to arrive at a final view of his work as a whole, we must see it as a reflection of deeper truths than any that can be described by a local and temporary picture of the cosmos, of psychology, or of the state.... (Spenser 1966, p. 22)

Moral idealism

Time and again we find critics escaping from the particular webs of Elsinore to what George Eliot termed 'that tempting range of relevancies called the universe' (1965, p. 170; Muir and Wells 1979, p. 16). That 'universe' is either 'ordered' or 'disordered', and tends to provide a springboard back to the prince: for Lily B. Campbell, for example, the play is an *exemplum* of revenge breeding a passion which is unamenable to reason and which is then justifiably punished (1930, pp. 143–4). This is again an argument which depends on a moralised model of a harmonically integrated universe being imposed on the personality of the prince. And, we might ask, what is wrong with private passion if it is directed against public corruption, what Brecht termed a 'long anger'? The notion of tragedy as moral fable, even if it accords with theory contemporary with Shakespeare, is, it seems to me, reductive. 'We . . . need to abandon any rigid moral stance, and to allow free intercourse between our moral notions and the great surge of fresh experience which is the play' (Knights 1979, p. 191).

Theological readings

Related readings are those which see the play as built around specific theological ideas. J. V. Cunningham's view of tragedy derives from his reading of what he takes to be Edgar's key line at the end of *King Lear*, 'Ripeness is all' [v.ii.11], so that the action of the plays is a manifestation of an inscrutable providence (1960; cf. Frye 1984, p. 254ff.). He places special emphasis on Hamlet's allusion to Matthew 10:29 in his speech to Horatio as he goes to encounter Laertes: 'There is a special providence in the fall of a sparrow. If it be now, 'tis not to come; if it be not to come, it will be now; if it be not now, yet it will come – the readiness is all' [v.ii.192–5]. But might these lines not be merely the index of a fatalistic state of mind rather than the motto of the play? Again some have taken Hamlet's view of himself as the heavenly powers' 'scourge and minister' [iii.iv.176] as an indication that Shakespeare saw Hamlet as a scourge of God, a divine agent, not necessarily good himself, who was sent to earth to chastise the evil (Elliott 1951). Dr Johnson concluded that 'Hamlet is, through the whole play, rather an instrument than an agent. After he has, by the stratagem of the play, convicted the king, he makes no attempt to punish him, and his death is at last effected by an incident which Hamlet has no part in producing' (1960, p. 112). But the line is spoken just after Hamlet has mistakenly killed Polonius, and may be delivered as much in anger as in submissiveness, as a protest against God's order rather than an assertion of it. Similarly H. D. F. Kitto, in a study which sees *Hamlet* as a religious drama like that of the Greeks, sees the prince as the paralysed victim of a contagious evil, 'a complexive, menacing spread of ruin' (1956, p. 337). 'Weeds can choke flowers. These weeds have choked Ophelia, and at last they choke Hamlet, because he could not do the coarse work of eradicating them. . . . So finely poised, so brittle a nature as Hamlet's, is

especially vulnerable to the destructive power of evil'
(pp. 327–8). These organic metaphors, although derived from
the play, do not do justice to a spectator's understanding of
the specific practices (the 'policy' in the Elizabethan sense)
that lead to catastrophe.

For the play is ironical: it postulates a higher level of
understanding in its audience than in the prince. This
prevents us from giving full assent to the thesis of D. G.
James, who is in danger of equating Shakespeare's point of
view with Hamlet's point of view and arguing that the play
is a manifestation of scepticism, a philosophical system
commonly studied by Shakespeare's contemporaries:
'Shakespeare's play,' he says, 'is an image of modernity, of
the soul without clear belief losing its way, and bringing itself
and others to great distress and finally to disaster'; it is 'a
tragedy not of excessive thought but of defeated thought',
and Hamlet himself is 'a man caught in ethical and
metaphysical uncertainties' (1951). Would (religious?) belief
have helped Hamlet?

At the end of the play Horatio breaks off his valediction
when he hears Fortinbras' drum:

> Good night sweet prince,
> And flights of angels sing thee to thy rest –
> Why does the drum come hither?
>
> [v.ii.338–40]

This is a typically Shakespearean moment. The divine
invocation is interrupted by political reality. The moment
cannot be, as Bradley wanted it to be, a sign that Hamlet's
essential goodness will be rewarded (1957, pp. 118, 140).
Rather, the juxtaposition of idea and reality (compare the
'dram of eale' and the entrance of the Ghost [iv.iv.35–8]) can
only induce sceptical detachment in the reader. As I. A.
Richards wrote,

> Tragedy is only possible to a mind which is for the moment agnostic or
> Manichean. The least touch of any theology which has a compensating
> Heaven to offer the tragic hero is fatal. That is why *Romeo and Juliet* is
> not a Tragedy in the sense in which *King Lear* is. (1924, p. 246)

Doubting wisely (see Donne's Third Satire) may be more

conducive to the writing of tragedy than the involuntary doubt invoked by James.

Criticism and social realism

All of these idealist critics, whether invoking a metaphysical idea of order or pointing to intellectual defeat for the hero, assume that tragedy is possessed of an essence (see Weitz 1965, p. 223ff., who questions this notion by invoking Wittgenstein's examples of language games). Bradley yet again: 'Let us attempt then to re-state the idea that the ultimate power in the tragic world is a moral order' (1957, p. 24). This may blind such critics to the particular facts of the play, blind them to the way different characters in the play might see the world in different ways, espouse different ideologies, blind them to the *differences* between *Hamlet* and similar plays of its period.

They may also be oblivious to the distinction between drama and theatre. What I have in mind is the following: it is indeed very difficult to read a text without imposing on it some sort of pattern, deriving from our own sort of order, without which our lives would be completely without meaning. One reason for going to the theatre is to open our minds to other orders, other emphases. Moreover, before we conclude that like us Shakespeare 'believed in order', we must remind ourselves that his *plays* were performed in *theatres* that were continually associated not with order but with disorder and sedition. They were often the sites of riots and frays (see the index entry 'Disorders at playhouses' in Chambers 1923). The companies of players, operating under aristocratic patronage, were in effect 'licensed', but served as perpetual embarrassments to the city authorities. In other words, theatres were in some respects like carnivals, occasions of institutionalised or ritualised riot (Stevenson 1985) that might not always be contained and which could spill out into a challenge to order (for an analysis of the literary carnivalesque, see Bristol 1985). (In this respect we might note how ceremonies, customs, and institutions within the play are violated or interrupted, 'more honoured in the

breach than the observance' – a point to be developed in
Part Two.) Out of this turmoil a *new* order may emerge, one
that might prove very discomforting to the sense of the
world, ordered or not, with which we as spectators or readers
started out on our experience of the play.

All this suggests a society open to a process of radical
change. It is this aspect of the play that has been inspected
by critics working within what we might loosely call the
Marxist tradition. Like Bradley, they take from Hegel and
stress conflict in the play, but, instead of seeing an idealised
resolution, they point to a new level of awareness in the
audience that will breed not fatalism born of mystification
but action. Eagleton relates the 'regressive states of being' of
the prince both to the psychological categories of Lacan and
to a familiar model of history: 'Hamlet is a radically
transitional figure, strung out between a traditional social
order to which he is marginal and a future epoch of achieved
bourgeois individualism which will surpass it' (Eagleton
1986, p. 74). Brecht, whose notion of the play as set in what
he called 'a valuable fracture point' between a feudal world
of chivalric honour and a Protestant rational world I have
already alluded to, wrote a sonnet about it (given here in the
translation by John Willett in Willett and Manheim 1976, II,
311):

On Shakespeare's Play *Hamlet*

Here is the body, puffy and inert
Where we can trace the virus of the mind.
How lost he seems among his steel-clad kind
This introspective sponger in a shirt.

Till they bring drums to wake him up again
As Fortinbras and all the fools he's found
March off to battle for that patch of ground
'Which is not tomb enough . . . to hide the slain'.

At this his too, too solid flesh sees red.
He feels he's hesitated long enough.
It's time to turn to (bloody) deeds instead.

> So we nod grimly when the play is done
> And they pronounce that he was of the stuff
> To prove 'most royally', 'had he been put on'.

Brecht, it will be seen, presumably takes his starting-point from Marcellus' description of the way that Denmark under Claudius has turned into an arsenal and is working day and night to prepare armaments for war [I.i.71ff.]. (Perhaps Claudius is following the advice of another politic usurper, Henry IV, that the way to keep the throne is 'to busy giddy minds with foreign quarrels' [2 *Henry IV*, IV.v.213–14].) Hamlet, so consumed with his private grief, is unable to perceive the true state of his country, and is awakened only by his chance encounter with Fortinbras, which produces not a conscious judicious action of justice but an impulsive and horrific slaughter. The action proves nothing except to make us afeared of the vendetta or militaristic honour: the true or best nature of princely responsibility and royal behaviour remains undefined.

Towards a feminist criticism

Let us now move from our analysis of the conflict between the hero and his world to another group of characters, the women in the play. We have already noted the dangers of abstracting the 'personality of the hero' from the text, and accordingly we would expect that there is little insight to be gained by simply talking about the personalities of the women. Nor do we seek to recover 'Shakespeare's own' views of them or of women: like so much else this information is irrecoverable (McLuskie, in Dollimore and Sinfield 1985, pp. 88–108). Instead we must look at the particular structures of power within the institution they inhabit, in this case the family. (Leverenz 1978 argues that Hamlet delays because he is entrapped between a patriarchal order deriving from the Ghost and his call for revenge, and womanly [*sic*] values of feeling and irrationality.)

To begin with Ophelia (see West 1958, pp. 17–32): she is subordinate to a patriarchy of three men – her father, her brother, and her lover, who is also a prince. We then must consult ideology, work out what images or constructions of women were prevalent at the time – as well as those that prevail among the modern critics that we read. (We may not be surprised if these, then and now, seem to total only two, angel or whore.) Laertes, we note, denies Ophelia's subjectivity: he assumes that Hamlet sees her only as a sexual object. Likewise her father will use her as an instrument in his designs, as a 'stale' or decoy. Polonius even says he will 'loose' his daughter to Hamlet [II.ii.160], a word used of setting a cow to a bull. So too he treats her as a commodity to be disposed of by sale: by a wilful play on words he takes Hamlet's '*tenders* for true pay / Which are not *sterling*' [I.iii.106–7, emphasis added]. Hamlet, having erected her to saint-like stature in his letter –

> Doubt thou the stars are fire,
> Doubt that the sun doth move,
> Doubt truth to be a liar,
> But never doubt I love
> [II.ii.115–18]

– embarrasses her intensely with sexual innuendo while they are watching 'The Mousetrap'. Are these vulgarities meant to be not overheard? – in which case they are a little less offensive. Are they meant to be overheard and therefore a manifestation of the prince's 'antic disposition'? Could they be played to suggest bawdy tenderness? Or are they simply a manifestation of his misogyny, his claim that all women are frail? (Jacques Lacan etymologises Ophelia as '*O phallos*' – 1977, pp. 11–52.)

Wherein does their frailty consist? Not simply in specific actions (Gertrude's unproven adultery [I.v.42] or connivance in the murder of her first husband) but in being sexually active or lustful, a charge [I.v.55] the Ghost lays to his widow [see Rose in Drakakis 1985]. Hence Hamlet's digression from his attack on Claudius to his attack on his mother's feelings for Claudius:

> You cannot call it love, for at your age
> The heyday in the blood is tame, it's humble,

> And waits upon the judgement; and what judgement
> Would step from this to this?
>
> [III.iv.68–71]

Coppélia Kahn, following through her observation that the Ghost is in fact a cuckold, points out that

> Viewed in this context, Hamlet's well-known misogyny and preoccupation with Gertrude's faults are an outlet for the range mingled with shame he feels at his father's situation. He must bury or disguise his awareness of it, because to admit it would damage severely his idealized image of that father. So long as he can blame a woman's frailty for the indignity his father suffers, as the conventions of cuckoldry enable him to do, that image can be saved.   (1981, p. 133)

Ophelia is at the centre of the contradiction. She and Hamlet had presumably been intimate – her songs suggest this. But her lover and her father treat her as a harlot, and we, like the Priest, can presume that 'her death was doubtful' [v.i.194], probably suicide. No wonder she found life intolerable, for, in the second part of the play, Hamlet seems to have been projecting his hatred of his mother's sexuality ('frailty') onto his lover and humiliating her too. (Hamlet's misogyny is in fact contagious. Hamlet is demonising Gertrude: for him, the something rotten in the state of Denmark may well be, we could conjecture, his own mother. Eliot and Dover Wilson too made women scapegoats: both stressed the guilt of the queen. According to the latter Gertrude was guilty of incest, and he explains away, and thereby excuses, Hamlet's vilification of Ophelia by adding a stage direction at II.ii.157 to bring Hamlet on early so that he overhears the plan to set Ophelia as a decoy. See Wilson 1934; 1951, p. 106ff.)

As so often, women suffer because they do not fit either of the two predominant images of women available. We can pursue these through two sequences: Gertrude's narrative of Ophelia's death and the songs of distraction. Millais captures the angelic Ophelia in his picture at the Tate Gallery of her floating serenely downstream. In death she represents the two ideals of women, sexual passivity ('ladies don't move') and, ultimately, silence. (Any articulate woman – Beatrice or Katherina – was branded a shrew.) Ophelia, though, had

chosen not to be silent: she sang (or 'went mad'). As we have
seen, Q1 indicates that in an early production Ophelia
brought in a lute. In 1965 Glenda Jackson, who played
Ophelia, 'the young, the beautiful, the harmless, and the
pious', as Dr Johnson called her (1960, p. 113), brought in a
guitar and turned Ophelia's sweet lays into songs of protest.

Language-based approaches

Genre and style

We might start by reminding ourselves of the crucial
Renaissance ideal of decorum. This may be defined as an
assumption that particular vocabularies and particular styles
were appropriate to particular genres. The genres were
generally those used by Greek and Roman writers. Elevated
genres, epic and tragedy, demanded to be written in a high
style; lesser genres, pastoral and satire for example, should
be dressed out in a middle or low style (Sidney 1973,
p. 133ff.; Puttenham 1589, p. 123ff.). It was, moreover, the
convention that these high styles should deal with people of
high 'degree' or social rank, which meant that the hierarchy
of genres reflected hierarchies in society. An author's choice
of particular words, therefore, might derive not from their
presumed exact relation to things in the world, but from a
word-hoard circumscribed by the genre that had been chosen,
and by the expectations of the audience. As Dr Johnson
wrote, 'Our opinion . . . of words, as of other things
arbitrarily and capriciously established, depends wholly upon
accident and custom' (1960, p. 9). Shakespeare, of course,
notoriously refused to be bound by the rules developed by his
neoclassic contemporaries, often writing what Sidney decried
as 'mongrel tragi-comedy' (1973, p. 135), but, like all
Renaissance writers, depended for many of his linguistic
effects on his audience's stylistic expectations.

Polonius reveals himself as a good neoclassic critic when
he objects to Hamlet's use of the word 'beautified' in his
letter to Ophelia: 'That's an ill phrase, a vile phrase,
"beautified" is a vile phrase' [ii.ii.110–11]. But what was
indecorous to the father might have been decorous to the

lover: Sidney in his *Arcadia* of 1580 had written, 'Thou art gone to a beautified heaven' (cited in *The Oxford English Dictionary*) – we cannot really tell, therefore, whether Hamlet thought of Ophelia as a lady painted an inch thick or not.

Decorum, of course, was an enabling rather than a restrictive practice (Hattaway 1982, p. 74ff.). Knowledge of a range of styles provided an author with an equivalent range of character types:

> there be that haue called stile, the image of man [*mentis character*] for man is but his minde, and as his minde is tempered and qualified, so are his speeches and language at large, and his inward conceits be the mettall of his minde, and his manner of vtterance the very warp & woofe of his conceits, more plaine, or busie and intricate, or otherwise affected after the rate.
>> (Puttenham 1589, p. 124; cf. Buffon's maxim 'le style est l'homme même' – style is the man)

Osric is a construct of his style: duplicitous because indecorous – he uses an ornate, encrusted, opaque style for a plain message.

In a famous *Rambler* essay of 1751 Dr Johnson, although always tolerant of the violation of generic rules, showed how sensitive he was to the violation of linguistic decorum. He was commenting on some lines in *Macbeth*:

> Come, thick night,
> And pall thee in the dunnest smoke of hell,
> That my keen knife see not the wound it makes,
> Nor heaven peep through the blanket of the dark,
> To cry, 'Hold, hold!'
>> [I.v.51–5]

> In this passage is exerted all the force of poetry, that force which calls new powers into being, which embodies sentiment and animates matter. . . . Yet the efficacy of this invocation is destroyed by the insertion of an epithet now seldom heard but in the stable, and *dun* night may come or go without any other notice than contempt . . . this sentiment is weakened by the name of an instrument used by butchers and cooks in the meanest employments; we do not immediately conceive that any crime of importance is to be committed with a *knife*; or who does not, at last, from the long habit of connecting a knife with sordid offices, feel aversion rather than terror. (Johnson 1960, p. 10)

Presumably he would have preferred Lady Macbeth to have called a knife a 'blade'. A less prescriptive critic might claim that modulations from one style to another can be an effective way of surprising or affecting the audience – as when Hamlet embarks on his bawdy interchange with Rosencrantz and Guildenstern.

That is one point of departure. Another is the Bible, where, in the book of Genesis, it is told how Adam gave the first names to creation and those names are their true names. Ever since Babel men have been striving to recover that knowledge, aware that there is no true or non-arbitrary relationship between words and things. A rose indeed by any other name does smell as sweet. Scientists need to devise new names for the compounds or processes they describe, for discovery is description, and the ascribing of 'true' names to things is a method of control over them. Our knowledge of reality is determined by the names we give to its parts and by the relationships between these names and other names in any given language.

It follows that when we are seeking to investigate words – not, of course, that all words are names – we should look not only 'through the text' to the things, real or imaginary, that they designate, but at the language or signifying-system in which they are used. (We may even want to argue that, as so few words can be said to be defined by what they refer to in the world, language tends to opacity rather than transparency – Nuttall 1983, p. 80ff.) Hamlet himself is aware of this:

> I know not seems.
> 'Tis not alone my inky cloak, good mother,
> Nor customary suits of solemn black,
> Nor windy suspiration of forced breath . . .
> Together with all forms, moods, shapes of grief
> That can denote me truly.
>
> [I.ii.76–83]

He is reminding his mother and the audience that there is a signifying-system or 'language' of behaviour that derives from customary courtly practice. For Hamlet, however, his sense of alienation from his world is such that he can no longer feel part of its practices, understand its signs or vocabulary.

This passage, taken together with our examination of Johnson's critical practice, reveals how discourse is formed by the culture in which it is created and how the language out of which it is created is inscribed with ideology. In Shakespeare studies this awareness impinges on our study of the practice of the textual criticism which we examined in the first section of this study. We might look anew at the ways in which neoclassic critics in particular 'corrected' the texts, often justifying their interventions on the specious grounds that there had been scribal or compositorian intervention in the process of transmission. In many cases their emendations derive from ideology, a theory of verisimilitude that derives from an ideological assumption about social hierarchy and a consequent notion of decorum that eschews the conceited metaphor, 'heterogeneous ideas yoked by violence together'. The phrase is Dr Johnson's; two of his notes, however, restore instances of indecorum that had been expunged by his contemporaries:

III.i.59. HAMLET. Or to take arms against a sea of troubles] [For 'against a sea' Warburton had suggested 'against assail'.] Mr. Pope proposed *siege*. I know not why there should be so much solicitude about this metaphor. Shakespeare breaks his metaphors often, and in this desultory speech there was less need of preserving them.

IV.v.84. KING. In hugger-mugger to inter him] All the modern editions that I have consulted give it,

> In private to inter him.

That the words now replaced are better, I do not undertake to prove; it is sufficient that they are Shakespeare's.   (1960, pp. 111–12)

Not that such ideological pressure is to be found only in the Augustan period: modern editors can reveal, even through the 'scholarly and objective' glosses they offer, something of the ideological assumptions they bring to their work. An example occurs in the gravedigger's scene. When Hamlet is handling the first skull thrown up from Ophelia's grave he comments, 'This might be my Lord Such-a-one . . . now my Lady Worm's, chopless, and knocked about . . . with a sexton's

spade. Here's fine *revolution,* and we had the trick to see't'
[v.i.70–6; emphasis added]. Edwards does not gloss
'revolution'; Jenkins offers 'as of the wheel of Fortune or the
whirligig of time'. Now it is true that the word 'revolution'
derives from the observation of celestial rotation, but its
immediate and particular context, embedded in imagery that
reminds us that man himself as well as death can be a great
leveller, makes us aware that the modern meaning, the
overthrow of an order or régime by those previously subject
to it (*OED,* sense 7) may be appropriate here. (Significantly,
perhaps, the first recorded use in the *OED* of the word with
this meaning dates from 1600, about a year before *Hamlet*
was written.)

Imagery

One particular form of language study which has been much
developed this century is that of words that are obviously not
names, but are 'tropes' or figures of speech, words that have
a more obvious connotative than denotative function, words
that function as 'images'. A pioneering study from the
modern period is that of Caroline Spurgeon, whose book
Shakespeare's Imagery and What it Tells Us appeared in 1935.
Miss Spurgeon listed the images in Shakespeare's texts and
arranged them into categories. She was thus able to point to
recurring images – clothing-images in *Macbeth,* images of
disease in *Hamlet.* Her aim was to psychoanalyse Shakespeare –
working from the romantic assumption that he was a mortal
possessed of an inward genius rather than a craftsman who
set out to build or construct. (Her approach is refined in
Armstrong 1946.) A more subtle approach that relates
imagery to characterization is found in the work of W. H.
Clemen, who points to the frequency of images from common
life in Hamlet's own speech:

> the wealth of realistic observation, or real objects, of associations taken
> from everyday life, is enough to prove that Hamlet is no abstract thinker
> and dreamer. As his imagery betrays to us, he is rather a man gifted
> with greater powers of observation than the others. He is capable of
> scanning reality with a keener eye and of penetrating the veil of
> semblance even to the very core of things.   (1951, p. 108)

The tables of imagery that were the result of Spurgeon's work led to a proliferation of thematic studies of the plays. (See above, pp. 52–3; for a sensitive and intelligent account of the themes of life and death, see Knights 1979, p. 28ff.; for an attack on thematic approaches, see Holloway 1961.) As I argued earlier, thematic studies, or 'spatial' readings of the plays (Knight 1960, p. 3ff.), do not fit our predominantly temporal experiencing of the unfolding of the plays (Booth 1969). More inappropriately, they can turn into studies of a play's 'atmosphere' (a key word in Bradley, incidentally), which generally settle on the text as a critical fog, blinding readers to details of action and social process, or they lead to bad productions which attempt to turn verbal or dramatic images into theatrical images – bathing the stage in red light in scenes where blood is mentioned, or setting *Hamlet* in an impractical 'nutshell-sized' set.

For an image need not be a picture, an encouragement to see what a word or phrase refers to in the mind's eye. We can see this by turning to Hamlet's key assertion in his first soliloquy that Denmark is

>   an unweeded garden
> That grows to seed, things rank and gross in nature
> Possess it merely.
>
> [ɪ.ii.135–7]

Working from this and the number of images of 'sickness, disease, or blemish of the body', Spurgeon saw the problem of *Hamlet*.

> *not as the problem of an individual at all*, but as something greater and even more mysterious, as a *condition* for which the individual is apparently not responsible, any more than the sick man is to blame for the cancer which strikes and devours him, but which, nevertheless, in its course and development, impartially and relentlessly, annihilates him and others, innocent and guilty alike. That is the tragedy of *Hamlet*, as it is, perhaps, the chief tragic mystery of life.   (1935, p. 319)

But just as Kitto who missed the irony of the play, equated Hamlet's view of the world with Shakespeare's view of the world, Miss Spurgeon's conclusion seems to me to founder on that reef as well as on more newly discovered rocks of linguistic theory. For, it seems, she is overlooking the fact that Hamlet is using a metaphor, and that a metaphor is composed of two parts, variously called tenor and vehicle, subject and object, or, more recently, signified and signifier. Now in this case Hamlet's conception of Denmark is what is signified, and the unweeded garden is the signifier. What is amiss in the state of Denmark, however, as Shakespeare makes obvious to the audience, is the consequence not of natural weed-like growth or of a transcendental 'condition', but of human practice at a specific historical moment: Claudius' usurpation of the throne and bed of the king of Denmark. Our attention as spectators, therefore, is directed not to what Hamlet sees but to what he constructs, the particular nature of his (imperfect) analysis of his predicament.

Hamlet, we have seen, was so unable to accept the decorum of Claudius' court that its very language seemed suspect to him. An example of his awareness of the problematic of denotation comes late in the play when, after discovering that he has been wounded by Laertes' envenomed rapier, he cries, 'Then, venom, to thy work' [v.ii.301]. It does make sense to say that the venom is at least partially responsible for Claudius' death – he is also stabbed and then forced to drink the poison intended for Hamlet – but it makes rather more sense to say that Hamlet is responsible for the death of Claudius. Hamlet casts himself as the signified, the signifier being 'venom'. The moment is profoundly ambiguous: Hamlet sense of self has been so invaded by the perversion of words that it is annihilated or transmuted to the opposite of itself. Alternatively we may wish to analyse the moment in moral terms and note that even at the end of the play Hamlet does not seem to want to take responsibility for his actions – they seem to be in the 'nature' of things. Or, by a third kind of analysis, we might say that Hamlet realises that he is caught up in a play which can be resolved only by the conventions of poetic justice, conventions which might not match the complexities thrown up by Hamlet's 'case of conscience'.

Language structures

Our examples serve to support the dictum that 'it is in the nature of language to be overlooked' (Louis Hjelmslev, quoted in Belsey 1980, p. 38) – a point that Hamlet makes to Polonius when he reminds him that what we read is 'words, words, words'. Aristotle had said that language was subordinate to plot and character, an assertion that many people would now want to challenge, and recent works on language have led us to investigate closely the notion of what has been called the 'classic realist text' – that is, the text that seems so 'life-like' that we tend to want to talk about its content, what it signifies, rather than the practices of signification of which it is constituted. Language, we have seen, may not be 'transparent'; rather it mediates between us and reality, interrogates reality even if it does not 'construct' reality (Nuttall 1983). (It is probable that Renaissance readers or audiences, steeped as they were in the study of rhetoric at school and university, would have been far more aware of an author's strategies of language and have taken a lively pleasure in his deployment of them. Or we might note that Shakespeare's language is itself marked by a high degree of self-consciousness – Elam, 1984.)

Different languages have different structures. In order to investigate these, most theorists in the field resort to the fundamental distinction made by Saussure between *langue* (a language system) and *parole* (speech or utterance) (Culler 1975, p. 8ff.). One language (*langue*) will differ from another. Users of computers will be familiar with the particular limitations of the different artificial languages or programs within which they work. 'Our knowledge of the world is shaped by the language that serves to represent it' (Norris 1982, p. 4). Moreover, we realise that each word or sign is defined not by its relationship to what it signifies but by arbitrary relationships to other signs within the system. It is for this reason that exact translation from one language to another is impossible, for only a limited number of words will have an exact equivalent. Eskimo has a multiplicity of words for snow; the African language Dinka has, I am told, 200 words for bull; French distinguishes between *fleuve* and *rivière*. Moreover, different languages have different grammars:

a tribe with a language that lacks a future tense would not be good at science because science has to do with predicting – or perhaps such a tribe does not have a future tense because the material conditions of its existence do not encourage it to make predictions.

Linguistic critics will attempt to describe the normative patterns or structures of a particular discourse. They might then describe the occasions when norms are departed from, when language draws attention to itself, is 'defamiliarised', is 'foregrounded' or is 'made strange' (Elam 1980, pp. 17–19). We have already seen one example of this when a word, the word 'words' itself, is repeated twice. Another example comes from Hamlet's riddling interjections at his first appearance:

CLAUDIUS.   But now my cousin Hamlet, and my son –
HAMLET.   A little more than kin, and less than kind.
CLAUDIUS.   How is it that the clouds still hang on you?
HAMLET.   Not so my lord, I am too much i' th' sun.
                                                    [I.ii.64–7]

The puns on 'kind' (kinsman and benevolent) and 'i' th' sun' (carelessly idle, close to the royal presence, treated by you as a son, dispossessed, in adversity – Jenkins 1982, long note on I.ii.67; Mahood 1957, pp. 111–29) threaten the decorum of the scene inscribed in the language practices on which the Danish establishment depends. The linguistic 'foregrounding' draws the spectators' attention away from what is signified to the means of signification, the patterns of relationship between the language (*langue*) and the social realities of the culture that employs it. (It may also represent an example of Hamlet 'hearing himself speak' – 's'entendre-parler', Derrida 1976, p. 98 – the beginning of the debilitating self-consciousness I shall examine in Part Two.)

Another example might be found in Claudius' prayer scene. Here we find the character engaging with himself in a kind of catechism as he wrestles with his conscience over the first Hamlet's death:

> What if this cursèd hand
> Were thicker than itself with brother's blood,
> Is there not rain enough in the sweet heavens

> To wash it white as snow? Whereto serves mercy
> But to confront the visage of offence?
> And what's in prayer but this two-fold force,
> To be forestallèd ere we come to fall,
> Or pardoned being down? Then I'll look up,
> My fault is past. . . .
>
> [III.iii.43–51]

Here we might feel that the order of discourse is violated, interrupted, by the pun 'I'll look up'. It could mean look up to God, the only source of pardon and salvation, but, as the words that follow indicate, it could also suggest that Claudius will stop praying, start to walk tall again on the assumption that he can proceed without the pardon of a God who seems to be simply the apex of a set of metaphors of rising and falling; proceed, in fact, to the plan of another murder, that of the second Hamlet.

If there can be a descriptive grammar of utterances, it follows, it is claimed, that there can be a grammar of narratives (Barthes 1977, p. 81). Instead of looking 'through' texts to enjoy 'rounded' characters we see 'behind' them, we pay attention to units of narrative in order to see the levels of meaning they generate. The interchange of the sentries in the first lines of the play provides our first example:

BERNARDO. Who's there?
FRANCISCO. Nay answer me. Stand and unfold yourself.
BERNARDO. Long live the king!
FRANCISCO. Bernardo?
BERNARDO. He.
FRANCISCO. You come most carefully upon your hour.
BERNARDO. 'Tis now struck twelve, get thee to bed, Francisco.
FRANCISCO. For this relief much thanks, 'tis bitter cold
And I am sick at heart.
BERNARDO. Have you had quiet guard?
FRANCISCO.   Not a mouse
stirring.

[I.i.1–11]

Here we note that order is disturbed as the relieving sentry challenges the man he comes to relieve, instead of *vice versa*. The *function* of the third line, however, is ambiguous: it might or might not be a password. We cannot tell, because the linguistic matrix in which such a formal utterance would be embedded is absent. As it stands, therefore, it could be taken as an example of dramatic irony, but an ambiguous one: it is open to the actor playing Bernardo, by his tone, to indicate that he is no willing servant of the new regime. Francisco's description of his feelings draws no response from his fellow soldier and thus functions proleptically to foreshadow the unexplained melancholy of Hamlet (Mahood 1957, p. 113). (We shall encounter another example of linguistic displacement in Part Two, when, in an analysis of the Pyrrhus speech, we examine the effect of epic pictorialism interrupting dramatic narrative.)

Language and ideology

Language cannot be value-free. Ideology, we now know, is inscribed in a language, particularly in the metaphors we live by. To return yet again to Hamlet's extended metaphor of the state as a garden, one of the elements of this utterance is an invocation of an idea of nature, here a wild, unruly, 'rank and gross' [I.ii.136] nature that cannot be controlled. One kind of analysis ('structuralist') encourages us to seek out the kind of *relationships* that define the meanings of the words used. The simplest form of structure that is basic to both natural and artificial languages and which children learn early in their mental development is binary opposition (Culler 1975, pp. 10–12). Now, the opposite of nature is culture (Derrida 1976, p. 103ff.), and it is a cultural phenomenon, usurped power, that Hamlet is examining. The metaphor of usurpation as a growth of weeds violates this category because it uses the terms of a natural organism – the idea of the state as a 'body politic' is another obvious example. Investigation of the binary opposition reminds us that there is nothing 'natural' about this metaphor (although its content or 'signified' may be 'the natural'): it is a mental construct. Moreover, if Claudius' power is identified with something natural, the implication is that it cannot be controlled. (The

idea of the state as a garden or as a body possessed of a
natural order can also be a useful weapon of social control – as
it is when, in *Coriolanus* (i.i.96ff.), Menenius uses it to justify
to the plebians the privileges enjoyed by the patriciate.)

A 'common-sense' notion of history, moreover, would lead
us to assume that nature is anterior to or produces culture –
we assume, confusedly, that 'culture' ('civilisation') emerges
as men evolve from their 'natural' state. The brief analysis I
have just performed indicates the contrary. The 'natural' is
not a historical condition but a political myth: the
investigation of language systems shows that nature is a
function of culture and not *vice versa*.

We can also approach again the feminist aspects of the
text, this time through language. Language, it is now
forcefully claimed, is *man*-made. The feminine is defined by
difference and, moreover, usually by attributing to the
female what is absent from the male (Spender 1985; Ruthven
1984). Within the category of the female the category of the
feminine is defined by further basic oppositions. The most
obvious is that of the opposition virgin/whore, which is a
combination of two binary oppositions. 'Virgin' can be used
in a value-free way to describe a girl who has not made love:
it is significant that there is no one word to describe its exact
opposite, although that is the state of most post-pubertal
women. In this respect there may be no unambiguous
linguistic place in our culture for the majority of women.
'Virgin' can also mean a saintly woman of high moral virtue,
and its opposite, whore, is a woman who sells her virtue – to
men or to a man who is not her husband. Women's goodness,
it seems, is determined by whether they are *virgines intactae* or
not. Any attribute of a woman that is unpleasing to men is
attributed to their sexual state. If they speak what they feel
instead of being silent, this must be, according to Hamlet,
the result of unlicensed sexual activity:

> I, the son of a dear father murderèd,
> Prompted to my revenge by heaven and hell.
> [note the opposition],
> Must like a whore unpack my heart with words,
> And fall a-cursing like a very drab,
> A scullion!   [ii.ii.536–9]

The Priest who is burying Ophelia is concerned that she might have committed what was then considered to be a mortal sin, and therefore be ineligible for burial in sanctified ground. However, like Hamlet, he does not concern himself with the possible facts of the case but dwells obsessively on the state of her hymen:

> Her death was doubtful,
> And but that great command o'ersways the order,
> She should in ground unsanctified have lodged
> Till the last trumpet. For charitable prayers,
> Shards, flints, and pebbles should be thrown on her.
> Yet here she is allowed her virgin crants
>   [garlands or chaplets],
> Her maiden strewments, and the bringing home
> Of bell and burial.
>
> [v.i.194–201]

Hamlet addresses his love as nymph [III.i.89], a word that ambiguously and insultingly combines the meanings of maiden and prostitute (*OED*, senses 2a, b; Partridge 1968, p. 154), just as the nunnery to which he would send her [III.i.119ff.] may well have been translated by his obsessions into its opposite, a brothel (a denotation in the slang of the time – *OED*, sense 1b).

Hierarchies of discourse

As has been recently pointed out, notably by Derrida (1976), it has been a feature of Western cultures to privilege the spoken over the written. We tend to assume that an aural encounter with the presence of a speaker or author gives us more meaning, a more 'authentic' experience, than reading his words. Which is why, perhaps, critics have tried to 'reconstitute' or 'reconstruct' the presence of the author in order to validate the meanings that they themselves have constructed out of texts. What does *Waiting for Godot* mean, we ask, and the myth of the author as source of meaning might encourage us, instead of attending to the way the play works, to approach Beckett for the answer. (He, of course, refuses, rightly, to reply.) In the case of *Hamlet* criticism it is notable how many writers have assumed that the soliloquies, endorsed by the tangible and 'authentic' presence of the speaker, represent sources of truth more profound than dialogues, where Hamlet's true 'self' may be thought to be more contaminated by his need to sustain a role. This assumption may be historically fallacious, as evidence would now suggest that soliloquies were not necessarily performed as if the speaker were in direct communion only with himself, but as rhetorical *acts*, speeches delivered directly to the audience in an attempt to persuade them to see the play from the player's point of view (Hattaway 1982, p. 88; Elam 1984, pp. 6–7).

Not only is the spoken privileged over the written, but the heard is privileged over the seen. Because Aristotle wrote that 'spectacle' is the least 'artistic' of the elements of tragedy, and because of a puritanical vein in English culture that devalues show, critics who have performed heroic feats in the exploration of Shakespeare's language have been notoriously slow to attempt to grapple with the theatrical as opposed to the dramatic, with what we see in the theatre as well as what we hear. It is for this reason that theatre history has until recently been regarded as a kind of antiquarianism, and only recently has a theory, semiotics (see below), been evolved to enable us to describe what we see in the theatre as well as what we hear.

Poetry, the discourse of tragedy, has long been privileged over prose, the discourse of comedy. Puttenham, like Sidney, claimed that poetic language had 'priority' over prose, evolved 'before any civil society was among men' (1589, p. 3). This was the academic view: practising writers knew better. Anthony Scoloker, writing in 1604, compared his *Diaphantus* to 'friendly Shakespeare's tragedies, where the comedian rides when the tragedian stands on tipto. Faith, it should please all, like Prince Hamlet' (cited in Ingleby 1932, I, 133).

One notable passage of prose in the play, the gravediggers' scene, has conventionally been labelled a source of 'comic relief'. Shakespeare himself may be said to have invited this: the stage directions and the speech prefixes of all three early editions (Q1, Q2 and F) designate these characters as 'clowns'. And yet our experience of this scene in the theatre does not necessarily encourage us to 'laugh at' the sexton and his mate. Rather they have some subtle if riddling analyses to make of whether or not Ophelia committed suicide – did she 'go to the water' or did the water 'come to her', i.e. did she fall? [see v.i.6ff.] – and brush up their threadbare pessimism with a sturdy egalitarianism (Adam was the first to bare arms [see v.i.31ff.]). We find that there may not be a distinction after all between clowns and fools, who, the Renaissance knew, could be divinely inspired or be licensed to speak truths unutterable by their betters. This category of varlets with straw in their hair, all too often given silly walks and Mummerset accents, are 'often given the most searching comments on the heroic action' (Heinemann 1985, p. 225).

Theatrical semiotics

Spoken language, of course, is only one of the signifying-systems used by a writer for the theatre. Just as there is a code of spoken language, there is a code of visual language (Elam 1980; Ubersfeld 1978). We don't just see a picture, we read it; and even at elementary level children must, for their own protection, be taught to decode the messages inscribed in, say, television advertisements. (Hamlet offers us a reading, although not necessary the only or the correct reading, of the play within the play – Alexander 1981, p. 92ff.) Not only are extended sequences readable in this way, but objects, the gestures of the players and the properties they use, are 'readable'. We can analyse the distance between us and a player: a player in close-up delivering an aside seems, by convention, to be 'speaking the truth', or, obversely, a player can draw attention to himself, if distant, by some extravagant gesture, and upstage or ironically undercut the discourse of a rival character. This kind of study is called proxemics (Elam 1980, p. 62ff.).

'Everything on a stage', it has been said, 'is a sign', or, putting it another way, every thing has metaphorical inverted commas around it (Elam, 1980, p. 8ff.). We do not see a throne; we see a 'throne' – the inverted commas reminding us that the actual throne is both a signifier and a signified, a utilitarian object for the use of the players and something that designates the source of power in Denmark or any state. In Trevor Nunn's Stratford production of 1970, Hamlet (Alan Howard), dressed in an ominous inky cape, leapt onto the player's stage at the end of 'The Mousetrap' and struck a pose which forecast his role later in the play as an exterminating angel. Later, in iv.iii, he was virtually stripped naked and punched savagely by the guards as Claudius sought to find where Polonius' body had been hidden. The removal of the cape seemed to signify Hamlet's shedding of his antic disposition: from then to the end of the play Hamlet's personality was identical with his role. (An exceedingly detailed 'dramatological score', a microscopic analysis of all the codes at play in the opening of *Hamlet*, is to be found in Elam – 1980, pp. 185–207.)

A tailpiece: those who believe that the world and indeed subjectivity are entirely constituted by language are moving in a very dangerous direction politically. In her book *Critical Practice* Catherine Belsey describes a Copernican revolution in the idea of the self (1980, p. 145): the old (bourgeois) ideal of the 'autonomous' self is dead. Instead, therefore, of seeking out particular individuals as the root of all evil – as Hamlet might have done, but didn't – we might seek out forms of ideologically constructed discourse. Pol Pot, leader of the Khmer Rouge in Kampuchia, was educated in this tradition. He eradicated what he took to be harmful intellectual components in his revolutionary ideology by attacking discourse. The means he used was to kill off the speakers of that discourse, eradicate the whole of the educated portion of a population. Shakespeare, as always, was prophetic: in *2 Henry VI* he has Jack Cade, leader of a popular uprising, give order for the hanging of the Clerk of Chartham because the poor fellow could read and write.

Part Two
Appraisal

Theatrical conditions

ANY CRITICAL ACCOUNT of a play ought to begin, I
believe, with some consideration of the theatrical conventions
that obtained when it was first produced. I shall begin there,
and then examine the way in which the play's structure is
inscribed in the consciousness of the characters, paying
attention to devices of interruption, defamiliarisation and
linguistic play. The thrust of my argument will be to
demonstrate the amount of ethical awareness the play
generates – awareness that is, contrary to the opinion of
many critics, shared in part by the hero – although I shall be
arguing equally that experience of the play does not generate
a moral conclusion.

In the case of English Renaissance drama, we are dealing
with plays written for stages equipped for spectacle but not
illusion. Theatrical spectacle – which in *Hamlet* depends not
on scenic devices but rather on large tableau-like scenes
created by players – may well, as the hero notes, have been
pleasing to the groundlings, but would not have encouraged
the wiser sort to take play for reality, the signifier for the
signified. *Hamlet* does not depend upon theatrical illusion,
upon the re-creation of the court of Elsinore at a specific
moment of history, and yet a good production demands great
attention not only to the inner life of the hero but to the
situations in which he finds himself. In this way it will
become a demonstration, to use a Brechtian notion, of the
way Hamlet's conscience (or consciousness) derives from the
interplay, to use Renaissance terms, of his fortunes with his
nature. Instead of watching inert historical chronicle and

tableaux – the native mode of the illusionistic stage – we watch ethical and psychological *analysis*.

Place on the Elizabethan stage was established by people, by players; settings or occasions were frequently created by rituals or ceremonies. In *Hamlet* these, as often as not, are interrupted: at the beginning of the play order is reversed as the new guard nervously challenges the old; the council meeting after Claudius's succession is dislocated by Hamlet's riddling interjections; the play scene ceases abruptly as the king walks out; the customary rites for a suicide are displaced by the makeshift rituals used at Ophelia's funeral, which are in turn violated by Hamlet grappling with Laertes; the duel between Hamlet and Laertes turns to a scuffle to the death after the prince discovers that the rapiers were poisoned; Horatio's valediction to Hamlet is disturbed by the drums of Fortinbras. These 'maimèd rites' not only signify that the time is out of joint, but also demonstrate the precariousness of power held by those who, like Elizabeth and James I, consolidated their rule by ceremony (James I 1888, p. 188; Williams 1979, p. 360). Playing the king well, maintaining an image of power, was so important that one form of the state in the early modern period might be properly termed a 'theatocracy'. In *Hamlet* decorum is constantly overthrown and, to quote the title of an essay by Montaigne, 'Fortune is oftentimes met withall in Pursuit of Reason' [I.xxxiii]: only in the idealised world of the players are we comforted by decorum, by seeing characters accord with their types. Only there does 'majesty demand tribute', and the adventurous knight (Hamlet's dream figure from a vanished feudal world of honour) 'use his foil and target' [II.ii.298].

It is also the case that, except for one and possibly two sequences,[2] the action takes place on one stage level. (We

[2] The two sequences where another stage level may have been used are the play scene, where the balcony could have been occupied by the audience of courtiers, and I.v.157ff. where the Ghost *'cries under the stage'*, in the 'cellarage'. This sequence may be played as comedy, which suggests, I think, that Shakespeare was pointing to the theatrical contrivance or game he was employing – with the intention of making us not only comprehend the ambiguous status of the Ghost (see Jenkins' long note to I.v.157) but realise that the prince thought himself caught up in a theatrical or unreal situation. The Ghost may incline Hamlet to particular action but does not compel him.

might compare *The Spanish Tragedy* or *Doctor Faustus*.) No supernatural agent intervenes from a gallery above to *compel* the action in a particular direction. This, I would claim, encourages us to a secular and sceptical reading of the play. In making this claim I am casting myself as Horatio-like critic, against a Hamlet who exclaims in what I take to be a mystificatory manner,

> There are more things in heaven and earth, Horatio,
> Than are dreamt of in your philosophy.
>
> [I.v.166–7]

Indeed, I would go so far as to argue that the play is imbued with agnosticism, that the hero's mind, in particular, is, as was once written of Kafka, 'strewn with the terrifying ruins of religious feeling'. The devil and God have been displaced, as we shall see, by the demonic figures of the Ghost and Pyrrhus.

Genre and theme

Hamlet is a revenge play. Such plays – like modern films about vigilantes – offered not only exciting plots but also, in Matthew Arnold's phrase, a criticism of life (1941, p. 4) in that they inquired how justice might be found if the court, the fountain of justice, was itself polluted (Belsey 1985, p. 112ff.). Orthodox thinkers of the period, following St Paul, argued that 'the powers that be are ordained of God' (Romans 13:1). What, however, if a bad king occupied the throne? Writers of homilies argued that no king must be killed, that the only course of action was to follow the example of Christ and his apostles and suffer passively (Belsey 1985, pp. 94–5, 110). As St Paul in the same passage had reported that the Lord said 'Vengeance is mine' (Romans 12:19), retribution must be left to divine intervention. However, as we have also seen, contemporaries were distinguishing regicide from tyrannicide, private vengeance from public vengeance.

Some few years after Shakespeare wrote *Hamlet* Bacon proclaimed, at the opening of his essay 'Of Revenge',

'Revenge is a kind of wild justice, which the more man's nature runs to, the more ought the law the weed it out.' The two clauses of the sentence reveal not only the customary contemporary abhorrence of the vendetta but a recognition that a desire for vengeance is 'natural' to one who feels he has been wronged. 'Kings must not be killed but in certain cases kings must be killed': Hamlet is impaled on the horns of a contradiction, and the main ethical dilemma for the hero and the spectators is to decide whether the task enjoined by the Ghost is a religious or political one – whether Hamlet is to be God's scourge in clearing out the impostumed corruption in the court of Denmark, or whether he is in bad faith, allowing a personal vendetta to become a motive for purposive, and casual, slaughter in the attempt to assassinate an elected monarch. (At the beginning of the play, moreover, Claudius seems to be a notable diplomat and peacemaker – Shakespeare is characteristically complicating the issue by inviting us to wonder whether a bad man might not be a good king.)

Dramatic structure

If that is the theme, we can approach it either through the character of the revenger or through the court. Shakespeare seems to have been willing to expend more than the usual theatrical resources to stage the court of Elsinore. 'Denmark's a prison', says Hamlet [II.ii.243], and, to create the claustrophobia Hamlet feels, the King's Men used not an oppressive set but a large number of players. (The point was made for modern audiences by the Soviet director Kozintsev, whose film of the play used very large numbers of extras in the court scenes – Jorgens 1977, p. 218ff.) Beside the soldiers, Horatio, Bernardo and Marcellus, Shakespeare gives us the court flies Reynaldo, Rosencrantz and Guildenstern, Osric and the Lord of v.ii.171ff., and the ambassadors Voltemand and Cornelius – the duplication of these last three roles suggests deliberate extravagance in casting. The duplication of these minor roles underscores the duplicity of the court. The incorporation of scenes such as the Reynaldo scene [II.i] inessential to the plot suggests that Shakespeare was much concerned to make Elsinore a place of intrigue, of spying and watching.

Now, we cannot know whether this is where Shakespeare's conception started. If we concede at least that his imagination may have been as much caught by the enclosed nutshell world of Elsinore as by the personality of the hero, we might argue that he made dramatic virtue and political interest out of the theatrical necessity of crowding the stage with minor characters. Moreover, not only did he expend resources on 'atmosphere', establishing the morality of the court, but, in the interests of making his theme prominent, he spent even more on what the rhetoricians called 'amplification' (Trousdale 1982) by giving us a trio of revengers, adding Laertes and Fortinbras, whom we are invited to compare and contrast with Hamlet. This reduplication of heroes, this gallery of types and anti-types – what the Renaissance called 'figures' (Auerbach 1959) – not only provides a set of interpretative cues for actors but also prevents identification with any one of the characters they play, so encouraging the audience to see the action from a multiplicity of perspectives. Our eyes will be, as Brecht said, on the course rather than on the end of the action (1964, p. 37). (This view of drama was not shared by Dr Johnson, whose Aristotelian overestimation of plot led him to complain that 'The action is indeed for the most part in continual progression, but there are some scenes which neither forward nor retard it' – 1960, p. 112.) We may infer, therefore, that Shakespeare's aim must have been to define, as clearly as possible, situation as well as character:

> So shall you hear
> Of carnal, bloody, and unnatural acts,
> Of accidental judgements, casual slaughters,
> Of deaths put on by cunning and forced cause,
> And in this upshot, purposes mistook
> Fall'n on th'inventors' heads.
>
> [v.ii.359–64]

A spectator at *Hamlet* is called upon to absorb more knowledge than is demanded by any of the other great tragedies – specific detail is more prominent than general statement (Trousdale 1982, p. 46). The play's structure is a pattern of analogies that alternately impinge on one another and are dissipated, with the result that, like the hero of the play, the spectator is tossed between what he knows and what he feels, as he tries to make sense of the experiences of the play and turn them into suitable shape for judgement.

Hamlet's own speeches, we are not surprised to find, are much concerned with definition through comparison, what Bacon in *The Advancement of Learning* called 'argument of contraries' [I.viii.3]. These are no mere riddles, indices of the 'nimbleness and flexibility of mind' that Bradley points to in Hamlet (1957, p. 120), but are tokens of the hero's strenuous moral deliberations. The pattern begins with his opening line: 'A little more than kin, and less than kind' [I.ii.65]. His father played Hyperion to Claudius' satyr [I.ii.140]. Is man a god or a beast? 'What a piece of work is a man . . . in apprehension how like a god: the beauty of the world, the paragon of animals – and yet, to me, what is this quintessence of dust?' [II.ii.286–90]. The adult 'common players' are compared with the 'little eyases', pigmy boy actors, in order to create a 'figure' of the falling-off from old Hamlet to Claudius [II.ii.309ff.]. Later, in the prayer scene: 'Why, this is hire and salary, not revenge' [III.iii.79]. To his mother (in a passage so beset with negatives that Hamlet seems to desire what he abhors): 'I essentially am not in madness, / But mad in craft' [III.iv.188–9]. After he has encountered Fortinbras:

> Rightly to be great
> Is not to stir without great argument,
> But greatly to find quarrel in a straw
> When honour's at the stake.
>   [IV.iv.53–6]

Even 'To be or not to be' [III.i.55ff.] is not just a soliloquy – the hero ruminating aloud – but an attempt to hammer out in the presence of the audience whether life consists in action or in mere sleeping and feeding [see IV.iv.35].

Patterns of analogy

We turn now to some larger defining comparisons. First, with Laertes who seems to have accepted the fallen state of Denmark in a way that Hamlet is unable to do. His advice to Ophelia is what we could call realistic: things and people do not match our ideas of them. The state of the nation dictates the state of the individual, a man's role in the state affects his character, so that a disjunction between seeming and being is inevitable in Elsinore:

> For nature crescent does not grow alone
> In thews and bulk, but as this temple waxes,
> The inward service of the mind and soul
> Grows wide withal. Perhaps he loves you now,
> And now no soil or cautel doth besmirch
> The virtue of his will; but you must fear,
> His greatness weighed, his will is not his own.
>
> [I.iii.11–17]

(The corollary of this realism, of course, is that Laertes tilts towards a quite unwarranted and prurient suspicion of Hamlet's idealistic love for his sister.)

Laertes' personality is defined further by contrast with Hamlet's in IV.vii:

CLAUDIUS.   . . . But to the quick of th'ulcer:
   Hamlet comes back; what would you undertake
   To show yourself *in deed* your father's son
   More than in words?
LAERTES.   To cut his throat i'th'church.
CLAUDIUS.   No place *indeed* should murder sanctuarize;
   Revenge should have no bounds.
[IV.vii.122–7, emphasis added]

We reflect how Hamlet, notably, had not cut Claudius' throat 'in church' in the prayer scene. The impulsive Laertes is an avenger 'in deed': the rhetorical figure called *ploche* (Puttenham 1589, p. 168), or repetition in a slightly different context, underlines his nature.

It is not just a question of comparing character with

character. One of the many virtues of John Barton's 1980
Stratford production was that it set family against family.
Polonius, Laertes, and Ophelia in that production were united
in bonds of natural affection – in contrast with the strains
and duplicities so evident in the royal house of Denmark.

Like Hamlet, Fortinbras, the second of the dramatic foils,
finds that his uncle has succeeded his father [i.ii.28]. Horatio
characterises him thus:

> young Fortinbras,
> Of unimprovèd [unrestrained] mettle *hot* and full,
> Hath in the skirts of Norway here and there
> Sharked up a list of lawless resolutes
> For food and diet to some enterprise
> That hath a stomach in't. . . .
>
> [i.i.95–100, emphasis added]

We have already seen (pp. 61–2) how Brecht used Fortinbras to
define the new and presumably militaristic order that will
succeed the peacemaking efforts of Claudius (King James's
motto was *Beati pacifici*). In terms of Renaissance humour
psychology, Fortinbras has the hot temperament of the
choleric man, while Hamlet is possessed of cold melancholy.
He is ambitious to pursue his revenge, but, as Hamlet acidly
points out in his defining comparison quoted above, he
confuses honour with dignity [cf. Hector in *Troilus and
Cressida*, ii.ii.193ff.] and has no care for the consequences of
his action:

> a delicate and tender prince,
> Whose spirit, with divine ambition puffed,
> Makes mouths at the invisible event [outcome],
> Exposing what is mortal and unsure ,
> To all that fortune, death, and danger dare,
> Even for an eggshell.
>
> [iv.iv.48–53]

An issue is being defined: does the end (the revenge of family
honour) justify the means ('The imminent death of twenty
thousand men' [iv.iv.60])?

There are also glimpses in the play of a fourth avenger,

Pyrrhus, who, in the speech Hamlet picks out of his memory, is seen avenging his father Achilles on grandsire Priam. The speech gives us a vision of an epic hero as the tragic mode of the play is first interrupted by Marlovian rhythms and then Hamlet's rendition of the lines is taken over by the First Player:

> The rugged Pyrrhus, he whose sable arms,
> Black as his purpose, did the night resemble
> When he lay couchèd in the ominous horse,
> Hath now this dread and black complexion smeared
> With heraldry more dismal. Head to foot
> Now is he total gules, horridly tricked
> With blood of fathers, mothers, daughters, sons
>   . . . Roasted in wrath and fire
> And thus o'ersizèd with coagulate gore,
> With eyes like carbuncles, the hellish Pyrrhus
> Old grandsire Priam seeks.
>
>   [II.ii.410–22]

The antique diction 'makes strange' (Shklovsky 1965, p. 18ff.) the presented figure. Like Hamlet, we encounter Pyrrhus in our mind's eye both as a fiction and as a reality – and the reality is a monster, the figure of a killing-machine totally without conscience, ready to mince the limbs of the husband of Hecuba, the 'mobled queen'. ('Mobled' means 'muffled': the word is brought into prominence through Hamlet's repetition of it, and so creates a 'figure' for the morally obtuse Gertrude.) Like Hamlet, Pyrrhus hesitates, and the frozen gesture creates an image that is obviously meant to emerge from Hamlet's consciousness:

> So, as a painted tyrant, Pyrrhus stood,
> And like a neutral to his will and matter,
> Did nothing.
>
>   [II.ii.438–40]

(At this moment in Wajda's production seen in Krakow in 1982 Hamlet began to speak in chorus with the Player as Pyrrhus' lines go on to describe how the thunder spoke in divine vindication of his act of vengeance. Only in fictions are wishes so easily fulfilled: in the world of Elsinore, Hamlet's reality and ours, the rest is silence.)

I may be guilty of overemphasising the importance of this sequence, but in my reading it becomes central to the play. (Harry Levin offers an analysis of the aesthetics of the speech – 1959, pp. 141–62.) Pyrrhus is, in Hamlet's mind, the half-comprehended mental antagonist of the Ghost, a 'broken image' [T. S. Eliot, *The Waste Land*, l.22] who hovers on the outskirts of Hamlet's memory, often undiscovered, but exercising a check on his actions:

> I do not know
> Why yet I live to say this thing's to do,
> Sith I have cause, and will, and strength, and means
> To do't.   [IV.iv.43–6]

By choosing Pyrrhus as a figure with whom Hamlet identifies himself Shakespeare *does* explore the moral problem of the revenger – this has often been denied (Waldock 1931, p. 25ff.; Brooke 1968, p. 191; Bayley 1981, p. 171). How is a man to be a revenger, executioner or assassin without being a murderer motivated only by 'hire and salary' [III.iii.79]. The ethical dilemma is explored through experience, the experience of this epic image, as much as by the 'contraries' of Hamlet's logic.

The conscience of the prince

This moral dilemma is made more difficult of resolution by Hamlet's coming to grips with the change in his fortunes that so radically affect the symbolic order or 'economic system of his psyche'. Not only is his father dead and his mother precipitately remarried so that he has, in another formulation of Lacan, 'lost the way of his desire' (1977, pp. 12, 14), but he has been displaced as heir-presumptive. Towards the end of the play he attempts to explain this to Horatio: Claudius, he says,

> hath killed the king and whored my mother,
> Popped in between th'election and my hopes . . .
>   [v.ii.64–5]

The metaphor in the second line suggests musical beds in a French farce. Even at this stage in the action, Hamlet cannot separate the private from the public, experience from idea, the sexual from the political. Those internalised figures of father and mother, authority and security, have been displaced. Under his father's reign Hamlet's role had been to uphold the order of the kingdom – and, besides, he had latterly lived away from Elsinore: now he is not only confronting a new peace-seeking settlement but his sexual identity has been shattered. After the visitation of a Ghost ardent for revenge, Hamlet is, as a malcontent revenger, fitfully aware that he is set to disturb the whole fabric of the court at a time when he is not yet ready to know himself.

Hamlet, of course, does not long remain innocent. Like Vindice, the hero of *The Revenger's Tragedy*, he becomes intrigued by murder, the means and not the end of revenge:

> For 'tis the sport to have the engineer
> Hoist with his own petar, an't shall go hard
> But I will delve one yard below their mines
> And blow them at the moon. Oh 'tis most sweet
> When in one line two crafts directly meet.
>
> [*Hamlet*, iii.iv.207–11]

We realise too that in Elizabethan usage 'antic' – in 'antic disposition' – meant not only innocently frolicsome (Antic, Frolic, and Fantastic are the names of three pages in Peele's *Old Wives Tale*), antique (as in the detail of Priam's 'antique sword' [ii.ii.427]) – with the suggestion that Hamlet at the beginning of the play sees himself as the hero of an old-fashioned tragedy of blood – but also monstrous: an antic headpiece turned a man into a beast in a mumming or a Morris dance. (Cf. Caesar's words 'This wild disguise hath almost/Anticked us all' [*Antony and Cleopatra*, ii.vii.124–5].) In some respects his role is that of the licensed jester, turning the jests of the charivari to earnest criticism of the grotesquerie that surrounds him (Bristol 1985, p. 187ff.). But all too often Hamlet seems to be using the conventional role of madman not only as a psychological safety valve but also as an excuse for cruel and unnatural behaviour.

Not only is Hamlet surrounded by people with roles

disconcertingly like his own – the subject is 'in a certain
position of dependence upon the signifier' (Lacan 1977,
p. 11) – but he is perpetually confronting the problem of
whether to trust the Ghost, who may be the devil in disguise
or whose words may be a creation of his fantasy. The play
exposes not only the paralysing effects of contradictory
awareness ('conscience') but, through the 'glimpses of the
moon' [I.iv.53] – Hamlet's restricted comprehension of the
totality of events in Elsinore – it leads us to the problem of
origins of knowledge (and of critical interpretation). That is
one movement, from experience to idea. There is another,
from idea to experience, in that Hamlet is commanded to
revenge not just by a ghost but by the ghost of his father.
The disputed authority of the Ghost is a figure for the
disputed authority of fathers – and this ghost, like Hamlet,
'is a figure consumed by torments of hatred' (Scofield 1980,
p. 141).

All these factors lead to psychological dilemma – it is not,
for a critic, I think, to attempt to *explain* this, but for
particular actors in particular productions to find *descriptions*
of the character which work for them. Suffice it to say at this
stage that at the beginning of the play Hamlet is in a state of
emotional turmoil, a state characterised by the alternation of
dark pondering and shows of wit. His black costume may
suggest he has found a role, but his gamut of verbal styles
suggests otherwise. When he might be establishing both a
new identity and new authority, his character, what he feels
himself to be, is always invaded by his role, what he 'seems'
[I.ii.76]. Because of the overpopulation of the Danish court
by extras, he feels that he is always being spied upon, 'too
much i'th'sun' [I.ii.67]. The Ghost is yet another spy, and a
reminder of old authority.

The division in himself caused by his moral dilemma is
compounded by his awareness that his very identity or
'attribute' [see I.iv.22] – which means, as Molly Mahood
(1957, p. 11) points out, both an inherent and an ascribed
quality – is jeopardised by the appearance in the latter part
of the play of others so like himself. (This sense of self-
monitoring is obscured in modern editions, which print
'myself', 'herself', etc., as one word rather than, as in
Renaissance texts, as two.) If his role is to be a revenger,

where is his authentic self? (In describing Hamlet thus I am setting myself against Dr Johnson, who wrote, 'Of the feigned madness of Hamlet there appears no adequate cause, for he does nothing which he might not have done with the reputation of sanity' – 1960, p. 112.) He could not be like Rosencrantz and Guildenstern, who are ready to 'give up [them]selves in the full bent . . . To be commanded' [ii.ii.30–2]. As Michael Pennington, who played the lead at Stratford in 1980, wrote,

> there are vertiginous switches in [Hamlet] from the humdrum to the hypermetaphorical and back which I could better understand when I saw that he sees himself simultaneously as a private man and also as a miscast avenging angel in some atavistic tragedy:

> Now could I drink hot blood,
> And do such bitter business as the day
> Would quake to look on. Soft! Now to my mother . . . .
> (Brockbank 1985, p. 121 [citing iii.ii.390–2])

Hamlet's awareness of indecorum – that Claudius is just a player king and that he himself is in no state to match his actions to his memory of his father's 'word' [i.v.110] (see Alexander 1971, p. 47ff.) – leads him to remember traditional meditations on the vanity of this world. This awareness emerges in reverie: in the graveyard scene when the prince reflects over the skull of his jester and draws up a list of those great men of whom nothing mortal remains. It can also be deduced from his assumption that the authentic or purposeful is the spontaneous or passionate (a notion further explored in the Player King's speech at iii.ii.181ff.). At the beginning of the play Hamlet is possessed of an engaging directness and naïveté with his friends (Bayley 1981, p. 168), an energetic sense of his own righteousness that can lead to casual threats of violence ('By heaven I'll make a ghost of him that lets me' [i.iv.85] – he is scarcely Coleridge's paralysed intellectual at this stage). But after the visitation of the Ghost his language can convert to wild and whirling words, and his relentless pursuit of the spontaneous turns to the cruelty that is revealed after he discovers he has murdered Polonius and in his plans to murder Rosencrantz and Guildenstern.

Even at the beginning of the play Hamlet feels that he is
an actor or player in a script he did not write himself –
'[these] are actions that a man might play' [i.ii.84]. Hamlet,
living in a Christian world, must feel at times as though he
was caught up in a Greek (and pagan) tragedy. (At the end
the indecorousness of Osric, a grotesque 'character', rouses
him to ill-suppressed fury.) In Greek, the verb *prassein*, 'to
do', means equally 'to be done to, to fare'. This is the
meaning for tragic action (*praxis*) that we should expect in
the world of Aeschylus, which believed that man was free
only to put on the harness of necessity. For Hamlet, acting in
the sense of doing remains painfully indistinguishable from
acting in the sense of playing. He is uniquely aware of the
way character and role, experience and knowledge, shape
and create one another. (We might say that Hamlet fails to
face squarely the moral ambiguity of revenge because, simply,
the task is not spontaneously taken on but imposed – and
perhaps because, like all sons, he has difficulty at times in
accepting the authority of his father.) If there is a 'problem'
in Hamlet's delay, this might derive not only from the
theatrical time Shakespeare had to expend in setting out the
case of conscience in all its fullness and with all its analogies,
but from Hamlet's desire to make his own actions seem
authentic to himself. (The distinction between 'theatrical
time' and the time of the action can be described by the
terms *sjuzet* ['plot'] and *fabula* ['story'] employed by the
Russian Formalists – Lemon and Reis 1965, pp. 120–2.)

Now it is apparent that 'The Mousetrap' is not just a plot
device but also a story, an image, that Hamlet reads or
explores, a 'mediated perception' (Alexander 1971, p. 92ff.).
Modern productions have, instead of showing embarrassment
with its quaint forms and inquiring, as of a naturalistic piece,
whether the king saw the dumbshow, turned the play within
the play from plot device into a central inquiry into Hamlet's
consciousness as well as into the authority of the Ghost
(Robson 1975). In the 1980 Stratford production that seemed
to enact the brilliant insights of his wife Anne Righter's book
Shakespeare and the Idea of the Play, John Barton foregrounded
the play within the play by placing a low stage upon the
stage from the opening of the performance (cf. Brockbank
1985, p. 115ff.). It almost completely covered the downstage

playing-area, and actors could do little without stepping 'on stage'. The device was particularly appropriate for I.ii, where both the protagonist Hamlet in his histrionic garb of black and his honest-seeming antagonist Claudius play cat and mouse, scrutinising each other's moves. Claudius is the voluntary impostor, Hamlet the involuntary one.

Details from 'The Mousetrap' itself show how it is used to render the consciousness of the hero. Lucianus, the villain, is, like Hamlet, nephew to the king. His speech that begins

> Thoughts black, hands apt, drugs fit, and time agreeing,
> Confederate season, else no creature seeing
>
> [III.ii.231–2]

suggests that in him, unlike Hamlet, form and cause are conjoined. He is able to suit his actions to his words [see III.ii.15], and able to work with the times ('confederate season') and unspied upon ('no creature seeing'). He is another projection of an idealised figure to set beside Pyrrhus. Hamlet's condition, therefore, compounds two well-known pathologies which are succinctly summed up in Freud's *Civilization and its Discontents*:

> There are cases in which parts of a person's own body, even portions of his own mental life – his perceptions, thoughts, and feelings – appear alien to him and as not belonging to his ego; there are other cases in which he ascribes to the external world things that clearly originate in his own ego and that ought to be acknowledged by it.   (1985, p. 253)

Varieties of ecstasy

Hamlet, then, is a man divided against himself. That, most of us would agree, although we may differ over whether this sense of alienation derives from a defect in his sensibility or, as Marxists would argue, from the dislocations in his world. It is reasonable to surmise that the division between his parents affected him grievously, although some might argue that his typically riddling account of this is the product of a neurosis:

HAMLET.   . . . Farewell dear mother.

CLAUDIUS.   Thy loving father, Hamlet.
HAMLET.   My mother. Father and mother is man and
wife, man and wife is one flesh, and so, my mother.
Come, for England.   [IV.iii.45–9]

Everyone remembers Ophelia's praise of Hamlet as man
of many parts, *uomo universale*, but for Hamlet this is an
intolerable number of parts to play:

> Oh what a noble mind is here o'erthrown!
> The courtier's, soldier's, scholar's, eye, tongue, sword,
> Th'expectancy and rose of the fair state,
> The glass of fashion and the mould of form,
> Th'observed of all observers, quite, quite down,
> And I of ladies most deject and wretched,
> That sucked the honey of his music vows,
> Now see that noble and most sovereign reason,
> Like sweet bells jangled, out of time and harsh;
> That unmatch'd form and feature of blown youth
> Blasted with ecstasy.
>   [III.i.144–54]

'Ecstasy' does not just mean 'madness', as Jenkins glosses,
but is a technical term designating a state in which the soul
has migrated outside the body, the sense familiar from
Donne's poem that bears the word as its title. Hamlet alludes
to the concept in another riddle: 'The body is with the king,
but the king is not with the body' [IV.ii.24], which suggests
not only, as we have seen, that Claudius, possessed like all
men of a 'body natural', is not the right head of the body
politic, but also that Hamlet feels a grim sympathy for his
antagonist, like him a man divided against himself.

   'The Murder of Gonzago' is interrupted by the exit of the
king before we see how the Player Queen reacts to Lucianus'
murder of her husband. We have seen how Shakespeare does
not make clear how involved the real queen Gertrude was in
the murder of her husband. Although Hamlet employed all
his ingenuity in the quaint device of the mousetrap to
establish the guilt of his uncle–stepfather, he seems to assume
without testing her that his mother is guilty, not necessarily
of murder, but of 'luxury' or lasciviousness. Just before the

entrance of the Ghost, Hamlet accuses his uncle of being a
player king, a shifty villain whose nature does not allow him
to play the role he has usurped:

> a vice of kings,
> A cutpurse of the empire and the rule,
> That from a shelf the precious diadem stole
> And put it in his pocket.
>
> GERTRUDE.   No more!

Enter GHOST.

> HAMLET.   A king of shreds and patches – . . . .
>   [III.iv.98–102]

We register, however, that Hamlet too is playing a part.
(Notice how, if the Ghost enters pat upon his cue, Hamlet's
next line could be taken ironically to refer to old Hamlet as
well as to Claudius.) He would be here the avenger, the cold
Pyrrhus-like killer. He has seemingly demonstrated this in
his precipitate despatching of the figure behind the arras and
will boast shortly of his ability to despatch Rosencrantz and
Guildenstern as they 'marshal [him] to knavery' [III.iv.206].
But the scene unfolds a relationship with his mother that is
at odds with this creation of his fantasy. His arrogant and
impertinent questioning of her ability to love –

> You cannot call it love, for at your age
> The heyday in the blood is tame, it's humble,
> And waits upon the judgement
>   [III.iv.68–70]

– and his pruriently vivid imaginings of the realities of her
marriage bed, couched in a syntax that reveals a pornographic
fascination with what he claims to recoil from –

> GERTRUDE.   What shall I do?
> HAMLET.   Not this by no means that I bid you do:
>   Let the bloat king tempt you again to bed,
>   Pinch wanton on your cheek, call you his mouse,
>   And let him for a pair of reechy kisses,

> Or paddling in your neck with his damned fingers,
> Make you to ravel all this matter out
>
> [III.iv.181–7]

– indicate a sensibility that is at best immaturely incestuous and at worst guilty of a customary demonising of the woman, his own mother.

We might argue that Hamlet is merely carrying out the instructions of the Ghost to work on her imagination when she is most vulnerable:

> Oh step between her and her fighting soul:
> Conceit in weakest bodies strongest works.
>
> [III.iv.112–13]

This is another 'ecstasy': Gertrude, according to the male view of her son and her first husband, has been 'deformed' by her actions – the Ghost does chide Hamlet for his tardiness but does not rebuke him for his misogyny. The possibility is raised, therefore, that the Ghost, although obviously in possession of the bare facts of the case, is actually a projection of the construction the 'ecstatic' (and therefore equally deformed) Hamlet puts upon them:

GERTRUDE.   To whom do you speak this?
HAMLET.   Do you see nothing there?
GERTRUDE.   Nothing at all, yet all that is I see.
HAMLET.   Nor did you nothing here?
GERTRUDE.   No, nothing but ourselves.
HAMLET.   Why, look you there – look how it steals away –
My father in his habit as he lived –
Look where he goes even now out at the portal.

Exit GHOST.

GERTRUDE.   This is the very coinage of your brain.
This bodiless creation ecstasy
Is very cunning in.

> [III.iv.130–40]

It is difficult to resist the conclusion that Hamlet is as

concerned to avenge himself upon his mother as upon his stepfather. (We saw in Part One, under 'Philosophical Approaches', how Ophelia, 'Divided from herself and her fair judgement' [iv.v.84], is a function of the language that defines her.)

Claudius too had to sustain a role. One of Machiavelli's great themes was that of the player king who maintained his power by maintaining his image, and we have already noted how well Claudius plays his role in the first part of the play. But, as with all Shakespeare's political players – Richard III is the most conspicuous example – his political duplicity insidiously destroys his sense of his own integrity and worth. Shakespeare, in fact, gives him a moment of tragic recognition, a speech that comes more from acceptance and understanding than any speech he gives to Hamlet, who, till the last, is still dwelling on his sense of his own riven personality in a manner that borders on equivocation ('If Hamlet from himself be tane away, / And when he's not himself does wrong Laertes, / Then Hamlet does it not' [v.ii.206–8]). The speech occurs in iv.vii when Claudius is ostensibly telling Laertes not to grieve too long for his father, but, it would seem to a sympathetic spectator, equally musing on the way that his own feelings for his new wife have turned to ashes:

> But that I know love is begun by time,
> And that I see, in passages of proof,
> Time qualifies the spark and fire of it.
> There lives within the very flame of love
> A kind of wick or snuff that will abate it,
> And nothing is at a like goodness still,
> For goodness, growing to a plurisy,
> Dies in his own too much.
>
> [iv.vii.110–17]

The scene is interestingly symmetrical, for, after bringing news of the death of Ophelia, Gertrude explores the image of her death by water in a manner that suggests that ceasing upon the instant with no pain would, for her, be the consummation devoutly to be wished. Perhaps this represents a half-awakening from the 'moral somnolence' (Scofield 1980, p. 171) which she exhibits through most of the play:

> Her clothes spread wide,
> And mermaid-like awhile they bore her up,
> Which time she chanted snatches of old lauds,
> As one incapable of her own distress,
> Or like a creature native and indued
> Unto that element.
>
> [IV.vii.175–80]

This repose of recognition contrasts with the frenetic and histrionic behaviour Hamlet displays in some productions that follow Q1 and call for him to leap into the grave at v.i.225 (Davison 1983, p. 15ff.).

Hamlet's habit of self-monitoring leads to his sense that the duel is both sword-play and another play in which he is merely bearing a role. (In 1965 at Stratford, Hamlet, played by David Warner, and Laertes fought to a pattern that seemed to re-create the pattern of the action of the whole play – cf. Scofield 1980, p. 179, on Kozintsev.) We see this in the way in which he embeds theatrical imagery in his commentary on the action. The sequence of metaphors begins when he is telling Horatio about his adventures:

> Being thus benetted round with villainies –
> Or [ere] I could make a prologue to my brains,
> They had begun the play.
>
> [v.ii.29–31]

It ends with his speech after the King's death:

> You that look pale, and tremble at this chance,
> That are but mutes or audience to this act . . . .
>
> [v.ii.313–14]

The metaphors remind us that to one pair of eyes the action might have been an execution, to another a murder. More than that, Hamlet's pursuit of the authentic seems to have been unsuccessful. In the sword-play the fighting turned to scuffling, and there is nothing to indicate divine intervention – if there is special providence at work, God remains obstinately hidden. For a crucial moment Hamlet acts spontaneously when he finds his sword has been poisoned. (It is this, not his father's command, that drives him to kill the king.) But, as he stabs, his words suggest that he is being acted upon: 'Then, venom, to thy work' [v.ii.301]. It is the poison, not Hamlet, the hero claims, that kills the king.

Once again he tries for authentic action and forces the king to drink the poisoned potion:

> Drink off thy potion. Is thy union here?
> Follow my mother.
>
> [v.ii.330–1]

'Union', as Bradley pointed out (1957, p. 122), is a powerful pun: the king's 'union-pearl', his marriage, and, perhaps the moment when Claudius' fate and Hamlet's role interlock. With regard to the stabbing, action is mere acting; with regard to the poisoning, justice seems to reside merely in the word and not in the world.

Othello's self-dramatising may be a case of the hero, as Eliot said (1951, p. 130), cheering himself up. Hamlet's depicts a case of conscience unresolved.

102

References

NOTE: here and in references in the text, dates of publication are those of the edition cited, not necessarily those of the first edition.

Alexander, Nigel, *Poison, Play, and Duel: A Study in 'Hamlet'* (London, 1971).

Armstrong, E. A., *Shakespeare's Imagination: A Study of the Psychology of Association and Inspiration* (London, 1946).

Arnold, Matthew, 'The Function of Criticism at the Present Time', in *Essays in Criticism: First Series* (London, 1911).

'The Study of Poetry', in *Essays in Criticism: Second Series* (London, 1941).

Auerbach, E., 'Figura', in *Scenes from the Drama of European Literature*, tr. R. Manheim (New York, 1959).

Bacon, Francis, *The Advancement of Learning*, ed. W. A. Wright (Oxford, 1900).

Barker, Francis, *The Tremulous Private Body* (London, 1984).

Barthes, Roland, 'Introduction to the Structural Analysis of Narratives' in *Image, Music, Text*, tr. Stephen Heath (New York, 1977).

Bayley, John, *Shakespeare and Tragedy* (London, 1981).

Belsey, Catherine, *Critical Practice* (London, 1980).

The Subject of Tragedy (London, 1985).

Booth, Stephen, 'On the Value of *Hamlet*', in N. Rabkin (ed.), *Reinterpretations of Elizabethan Drama* (New York, 1969) pp. 137–76.

Bradley, A. C., *Shakespearean Tragedy* (London, 1957).

Brecht, Bertolt, *Brecht on Theatre*, tr. John Willett (London, 1964).

Messingkauf Dialogues, tr. John Willett (London, 1977).

Bristol, Michael D., *Carnival and Theater* (New York, 1985).

Brockbank, Philip (ed.), *Players of Shakespeare* (Cambridge, 1985).

Brooke, Nicholas, *Shakespeare's Early Tragedies* (London, 1968).

Bullough, G., *Narrative and Dramatic Sources of Shakespeare*, VII (London, 1973).

Campbell, Lily B., *Shakespeare's Tragic Heroes: Slaves of Passion* (Cambridge, 1930).

Certain Sermons or Homilies (Oxford, 1822).

Chambers, E. K., *The Elizabethan Stage*, 4 vols (Oxford, 1923).

Clemen, W. H., *The Development of Shakespeare's Imagery* (London, 1951).

Coleridge, S. T., *Coleridge's Essays and Lectures on Shakespeare*, Everyman edn (London, n.d.).

Culler, Jonathan, *Structuralist Poetics* (London, 1975).

Cunningham, J. V., *Woe or Wonder* (Chicago, 1960).

Davison, Peter, *Hamlet: Text and Performance* (London, 1983).

Derrida, Jacques, *Of Grammatology*, tr. Gayatri Spivack (Baltimore, 1976).

Dessen, Alan C., *Elizabethan Stage Conventions* (Cambridge, 1984).

Dickens, Charles, *Great Expectations*, Penguin edn (Harmondsworth, 1965).

Dillon, George L., 'Complexity and Change of Character in Neo-Classical Criticism', *Journal of the History of Ideas*, xxxv (1974) 51–61.

Dollimore, Jonathan, *Radical Tragedy: Religion, Ideology and Power in the Drama of Shakespeare and his Contemporaries* (Brighton, 1984).

Dollimore, J., and Sinfield, A. (eds), *Political Shakespeare* (Manchester, 1985).

Donaldson, Ian (ed.), *Ben Jonson*, The Oxford Authors (Oxford, 1985).

Drakakis, J. (ed.), *Alternative Shakespeares* (London, 1985).

Eagleton, Terry, *Marxism and Literary Criticism* (London, 1976). *William Shakespeare* (Oxford, 1986).

Edwards, Philip (ed.), *Hamlet*, New Cambridge Shakespeare (Cambridge, 1985).

Elam, Keir, *The Semiotics of Theatre and Drama* (London, 1980). *Shakespeare's Universe of Discourse* (Cambridge, 1984).

Eliot, George, *Middlemarch*, Penguin edn (Harmondsworth, 1965).

Eliot, T. S., 'Hamlet' (1919), in *Selected Essays* (London, 1951) pp. 141–7.

Elliott, G. R., *Scourge and Minister: A Study of 'Hamlet' as a Tragedy of Revengefulness and Justice* (Durham, NC, 1951).

Ellis, David, and Mills, Howard, 'Romanticizing and Self-Identification in Coleridge's Hamlet: The Notes versus the Lectures', *Essays in Criticism*, xxix (1979) 244–53.

Fergusson, Francis, *The Idea of a Theater* (New York, 1953).

Foakes, R. A., 'The Art of Cruelty: Hamlet and Vindice', *Shakespeare Survey*, XXVI (1973).

Freud, Sigmund, *The Interpretation of Dreams* (London, 1914). *The Standard Edition of the Complete Psychological Works of Sigmund Freud*, ed. James Strachey *et al.*, IV (London, 1953). *Civilization, Society and Religion*, Pelican Freud Library, XII (Harmondsworth, 1985).

Frye, R. M., *The Renaissance 'Hamlet': Issues and Responses in 1600* (Princeton, NJ, 1984).

Granville-Barker, Harley, *Prefaces to Shakespeare* (London, 1972).

Hattaway, Michael, *Elizabethan Popular Theatre* (London, 1982).

Hazlitt, William, *Characters of Shakespear's Plays* (London, 1817).

Hegel, G. W. F., *Hegel on Tragedy*, ed. Anne and Henry Paolucci (New York, 1975).

Heinemann, Margot, 'How Brecht Read Shakespeare', in Dollimore and Sinfield (1985).

Holloway, John, *The Story of the Night* (London, 1961).

Honigmann, E., *Shakespeare: The 'Lost Years'* (Manchester, 1985).

Ingleby, C. M., *et al.*, *The Shakspere Allusion-Book*, 2 vols (London, 1932).

Jacobson, Howard, and Sanders, Wilbur, *Shakespeare's Magnanimity* (London, 1978).

James I, *The Basilikon Doron of King James I*, in H. Morley (ed.), *A Miscellany* (London, 1888).

James, D. G., *The Dream of Learning* (Oxford, 1951).

Jenkins, Harold, '*Hamlet* Then till Now' (1965), in Kenneth Muir and Stanley Wells (eds), *Aspects of 'Hamlet'* (Cambridge, 1979).
    (ed.), *Hamlet*, New Arden Shakespeare (London, 1982).

Johnson, Jerali, 'The Concept of the King's Two Bodies in *Hamlet*', *Shakespeare Quarterly*, XVIII (1967) 430–4.

Johnson, Samuel, *Samuel Johnson on Shakespeare*, ed. W. K. Wimsatt (New York, 1960).

Jones, Ernest, *Hamlet and Oedipus* (Garden City, NY, 1949).

Jones, John, *On Aristotle and Greek Tragedy* (London, 1962).

Jorgens, Jack J., *Shakespeare on Film* (Bloomington, Ind., 1977).

Kahn, Coppélia, *Masculine Identity in Shakespeare* (Berkeley, Calif., 1981).

Kettle, Arnold, 'From *Hamlet* to *Lear*', in A. Kettle (ed.), *Shakespeare in a Changing World* (London, 1964).

Kitto, H. D. F., *Form and Meaning in Drama* (London, 1956).

Klibansky, R., Panofsky, E., and Saxl, F., *Saturn and Melancholy* (London, 1964).

Knight, G. Wilson, *The Wheel of Fire* (London, 1960).

Knights, L. C., *'Hamlet' and other Shakespearean Essays* (Cambridge, 1979).

Lacan, Jacques, 'Desire and the Interpretation of Desire in *Hamlet*', *Yale French Studies*, 55–6 (1977) 11–52.

Lawrence, D. H., *Twilight in Italy*, Penguin edn (Harmondsworth, 1960 ed.).

Lemon, Lee T., and Reis, Marion J., *Russian Formalist Criticism* (Lincoln, Nebr., and London, 1965).

Leverenz, David, 'The Woman in Hamlet: An Interpersonal View', *Signs*, 4 (1978) 291–308.

Levin, Harry, *The Question of Hamlet* (New York, 1959).

Levin, Richard, *New Readings vs. Old Plays* (Chicago, 1979).

Lewis, C. S., 'Hamlet: the Prince or the Poem', *Proceedings of the British Academy*, xxviii (1942) 147–52.

Lidz, Theodore, *Hamlet's Enemy: Madness and Myth in 'Hamlet'* (New York, 1975).

McGann, Jerome J., *A Critique of Modern Textual Criticism* (Chicago, 1983).

    The Beauty of Inflections (Oxford, 1985).

Mahood, M. M., *Shakespeare's Wordplay* (London, 1957).

Marsh, Derick, *Shakespeare's 'Hamlet'* (Sydney, 1970).

Marx, Karl, *Selected Works* (London, 1968).

Meyerhold, Vsevolod, *Meyerhold on Theatre*, ed. Edward Braun (London, 1969).

Miller, Jonathan, *Subsequent Performances* (London, 1986).

Montaigne, Michel de, *Essayes*, tr. John Florio (1603), 3 vols ([London], 1910).

Muir, Kenneth, *The Sources of Shakespeare's Plays* (London, 1977).

Muir, Kenneth, and Wells, Stanley (eds), *Aspects of 'Hamlet'* (Cambridge, 1979).

Murray, Gilbert, *Hamlet and Orestes* (London, 1914).

Norris, Christopher, *Deconstruction: Theory and Practice* (London, 1982).

Nuttall, A. D., *A New Mimesis: Shakespeare and the Representation of Reality* (London, 1983).

Parker, Patricia, and Hartman, Geoffrey (eds), *Shakespeare and the Question of Theory* (London, 1985).

Partridge, Eric, *Shakespeare's Bawdy* (London, 1968).

Powell, Raymond, *Shakespeare and the Critics' Debate* (London, 1980).

Prosser, Eleanor, *Hamlet and Revenge* (London, 1967).

Puttenham, George, *The Arte of English Poesie* (London, 1589).

Richards, I. A., *Principles of Literary Criticism* (London, 1924).

Robson, W. W., 'Did the King see the Dumb Show?', *Cambridge Quarterly*, VI (1975).

Rose, Elliot, *Cases of Conscience* (Cambridge, 1975).

Ruthven, R. K., *Critical Assumptions* (Cambridge, 1979).

    Feminist Literary Studies (Cambridge, 1984).

Schanzer, E., *The Problem Plays of Shakespeare* (New York, 1965).

Scofield, Martin, *The Ghosts of 'Hamlet'* (Cambridge, 1980).

Shklovsky, Victor, 'Art as Technique', in Lemon and Reis (1965).

Sidney, Sir Philip, *An Apology for Poetry*, ed. G. Shepherd (Manchester, 1973).

Spender, Dale, *Man Made Language* (London, 1985).

Spenser, Theodore, *Shakespeare and the Nature of Man* (London, 1966).

Spurgeon, Caroline, *Shakespeare's Imagery and What it Tells Us* (Cambridge, 1935).

Stauffer, Donald A., *Shakespeare's World of Images* (Bloomington, Ind., 1966).

Stevenson, J., 'The "Moral Economy" of the English Crowd: Myth and Reality', in Anthony Fletcher and John Stevenson (eds), *Order and Disorder in Early Modern England* (Cambridge, 1985) 218–38.

Stewart, J. I. M., *Character and Motive in Shakespeare* (London, 1949).

Stoll, E. E., *Hamlet: An Historical and Comparative Study*, Research Publications of the University of Minnesota, VIII (1919).

Thomas, Keith, *Religion and the Decline of Magic*, Penguin edn (Harmondsworth, 1973).

Tillyard, E. M. W., *The Elizabethan World Picture* (London, 1943).

    Shakespeare's Problem Plays (London, 1964).

Trousdale, Marion, *Shakespeare and the Rhetoricians* (London, 1982).

Ubersfeld, Anne, *Lire le théâtre* (Paris, 1978).

Voltaire, F.-M. A., *Dissertation sur la tragédie ancienne et moderne* (Paris, 1749).

Waldock, A. J. A., *Hamlet: A Study in Critical Method* (Cambridge, 1931).

Weimann, Robert, 'Mimesis in *Hamlet*', in Parker and Hartman (1985).

Weitz, Morris, *'Hamlet' and the Philosophy of Literary Criticism* (London, 1965).

Wellek, René, 'A. C. Bradley, Shakespeare, and the Infinite', *Philological Quarterly*, LIV (1975) 85–103.

West, Rebecca, *The Court and the Castle* (New Haven, Conn., 1958).

Willett, John, and Manheim, Ralph (eds), *Bertolt Brecht Poems* (London, 1976).

Williams, Penry, *The Tudor Regime* (Oxford, 1979).

Williams, Raymond, *Marxism and Literature* (Oxford, 1977).

Wilson, J. Dover, *What Happens in 'Hamlet'* (Cambridge, 1951).

    The Essential Shakespeare (Cambridge, 1952).

    (ed.), *Hamlet* (Cambridge, 1934).

Wimsatt, W. K., and Brooks, Cleanth, *Literary Criticism: A Short History* (New York, 1957).

Wittgenstein, L., *Lectures and Conversations*, ed. Cyril Barrett (Berkeley, 1966).

Wrightson, Keith, *English Society 1580–1680* (London, 1982).

Yates, Frances, *The Occult Philosophy in the Elizabethan Age* (London, 1983).

Further Reading

THE FOLLOWING is a short guide to some of the most useful books and articles for those wishing to pursue study of the play and the responses it has evoked.

Alexander, Nigel, *Poison, Play, and Duel: A Study in 'Hamlet'* (London, 1971).

Booth, Stephen, 'On the Value of *Hamlet*', in N. Rabkin (ed.), *Reinterpretations of Elizabethan Drama* (New York, 1969) pp. 137–76.

Davison, Peter, *'Hamlet': Text and Performance* (London, 1983).

Dollimore, Jonathan, *Radical Tragedy: Religion, Ideology and Power in the Drama of Shakespeare and his Contemporaries* (Brighton, 1984).

Frye, R. M., *The Renaissance 'Hamlet': Issues and Responses in 1600* (Princeton, NJ, 1984).

Jump, John (ed.), *Hamlet*, Casebook series (London, 1968).

Knights, L. C., *'Hamlet' and other Shakespearean Essays* (Cambridge, 1979).

Lawrence, D. H., 'The Theatre', in *Twilight in Italy*, Penguin edn (Harmondsworth, 1960).

Mahood, M. M., *Shakespeare's Wordplay* (London, 1957).

Muir, Kenneth, and Wells, Stanley (eds), *Aspects of 'Hamlet'* (Cambridge, 1979).

Robson, W. W., 'Did the King see the Dumb Show?', *Cambridge Quarterly*, VI (1975).

Scofield, Martin, *The Ghosts of 'Hamlet'* (Cambridge, 1980).

Index